Understanding
is the Key

A Comprehensive Guide to Creating a Partnership for Life with Your Young Horse

By Gabriele Neurohr

Dedication

To you, the horse owner with a dream: This horse dream deserves to be fulfilled because horses fill our life and heart with magic despite all the tears, money and effort we put in. I dedicate this book to YOU, to help YOU reach your dream of a fulfilling relationship with this wonderful being, your horse.

To my parents, who taught me that true happiness is found in following and fulfilling your dream, not necessarily in money. Thank you for always having supported me with so much love!

To Marie-Claire de Selliers, who supported me wherever she could to learn and grow. She gave me the opportunity to work and gain the necessary experience at her wonderful stables in the middle of France. The thankfulness I have can't be expressed with words.

To my most influential mentor, Berni Zambail, who showed me the way to the heart of my horse, Mazirah. He showed me how to listen to horses with an open heart and to have a relationship based on understanding each other.

To my husband, who always believes in me and supports me and my crazy vision of dedicating my life to my love for horses and sharing it with others.

To my horses, who fill my life with magic, joy and happiness. I thank them all for helping me become who I am today.

CONTENTS

Foreword

by Berni Zambail

Young Horse Development Specialist,
Success Coach for Horse and Human

I spent my life with horses, first as a farrier, then as a full-time horse trainer and instructor. I had the honor to ride and learn with many well-known masters of horsemanship, such as Pat Parelli, Alfonso Aguilar, Desmond O'Brien, Walter Zettel, Dr Bob Miller, Mike Bridges, Bent Branderup, Manolo Oliva, Luis Lucio and Pedro Torres to name just a few.

One topic close to my heart was always the education of young horses, from newborn foal all the way through foundation training and specialization. In my daily work today as a coach for horse owners, I get to see again and again how the dream of educating and creating a special relationship with the young horse ends in a nightmare. This was usually when people called me and asked for help to fix their young horse who had become a problem horse. The question is why does it even come to this point?

I believe it is because most people aren't really aware of what it takes to own a horse, let alone to educate a young horse from scratch. Often, I see people just running blindly behind a dream, acting out of impulse without keeping the big picture in mind. At some point, the young-horse owners realizes they can't keep up with their horse's needs; they find out that they don't know enough to keep up with all the challenges a young horse presents every day. They find themselves caught in a cycle of overwhelm and frustration. I believe this could be avoided if people armed themselves with the right knowledge and mindset upfront. I know that Gabi feels the same way.

I got to know Gabi and her mare, Mazirah, in 2007 when she became my student. She found herself in a dilemma with the young, spirited mare, bought as a green three-year-old, whom Gabi wanted to educate all by herself. Of course, at first, she was one of those cases I described above, but she did what was necessary to make her dream a reality. She came to me with an open mind and heart to learn what it takes to reach her horse's heart. I shared with her my experience and knowledge, especially about educating the young horse and setting it up to live a comfortable and happy life in the human world. Gabi continued to follow her passion, learning to understand the horse's mind and heart, and she is now a very experienced trainer for horse-human couples. She speaks from my heart in this book.

After reading this book, you will know exactly what kind of adventure awaits you with your young horse. Gabi gives you all the keys you need to unlock the doors to make owning a young horse your dream, rather than a nightmare. I recommend this book to anyone who wants to build a solid and happy relationship that lasts with a young horse, based on connection, trust and mutual respect. I wish you many helpful insights when reading this book and especially many, many happy hours with your horse!

Introduction

I was born with horses in my DNA. My father wasn't a famous show jumper and my mother didn't teach lessons in a pony club. Nobody in my family was involved in horses until they gave in to my begging. Somehow, I was always magically drawn to horses.

I wrote this book for women like me, who have a young horse and want to create a happy and reliable partner they can spend many happy years with. If your goal is that your horse enjoys the time you spend together just as much as you but, at the same time, is well educated and reliable, this book will give you the keys to achieve just that. Before I tell you what this book contains, let me first tell you what you WON'T find here.

This book is not just another method of training horses. Success with horses really isn't about methods; it's about understanding the principles of horse training. Every horse is unique, and that's why so often off-the-shelf methods don't work for every horse.

This book is not about fixing your horse's problems. But it will help you to avoid having problems in the first place because you will understand where all the problems we encounter often originate.

This book is not a detailed how-to-educate-your-horse manual, yet it will enable you to create a solid master plan to train your young horse into a happy and reliable partner for a lifetime.

This book is not a follow-your-fairy-tale-horse-dream, just-go-for-it book because that would be irresponsible! However, this book will provide you the knowledge you need to bring you closer to fulfilling your dream with your horse.

This book is also not a dry, science-based psychology book where you end up with cramps in your brain, questioning even more whether you are doing things right. But this book will give you a deep understanding of how horses learn and think and how you can apply the knowledge easily into everyday life with your horse.

Young horse, high responsibility

You might have bought a young horse because you want to start with a clean slate, be in charge of his education and grow together. Maybe you have already had negative experiences owning a horse with bad habits that came with some emotional baggage. Now you aim to prevent the same thing from happening again and make sure that your horse has no bad experiences. Your goal might be to develop not only a well-educated and reliable partner for a lifetime but also an especially unique and happy relationship with your horse. Maybe the horse you have right now is old and you want to slowly bring on your new partner. Whatever your reason for having a young horse, the journey ahead will be filled with joy.

Naturally, having a young horse comes with a high sense of responsibility. We don't want to mess anything up. You might have heard many professionals say that a young horse is not for an amateur rider and that you should better get an older, seasoned horse. But there you are, with your youngster and so many questions on your mind that you would love to have answered. Yes, you might not have the experience of a professional. Fortunately, you have other assets on your side: your good will to do everything right, as well as your enthusiasm and love for this project. I understand you so well.

My own search for a roadmap

I remember clearly when I had just bought Mazirah, shortly after I turned seventeen. She was a sensitive three-year-old Shagya-Arabian mare. I was full of enthusiasm, hope, ideas and good will to do everything right for her. I didn't have much money, but I invested every cent I had buying books of reputable horse trainers, including Monty Roberts, Linda Tellington Jones, Richard Maxwell, Klaus Ferdinand Hempfling and many others.

I had so many questions and was looking for a roadmap to show me how to develop my little mare into my future dream horse. What should I teach? In what order should I teach the tasks? Am I doing too much or too little? What do I have to look out for? How do I know if I can go to the next step? What do I do when things don't work? How does a horse learn and how can I adapt to my horse's unique nature? How can I set up the session in a way that Mazirah will enjoy learning and spending time with me? My number-one goal was for us to become true friends and for her to want to do stuff with me.

Yet, so many of my questions weren't answered by any of the books I read. I needed a real roadmap I could actually put to use with my abilities of an amateur. Some books gave me the how-to for some exercises, but the problem was that the method described often didn't work because Mazirah wasn't like the horse described in the book.

We progressed little by little over our first summer together. Soon, I started to take her on trail rides, as I had no arena. This is when she started to become very defensive and emotional. She was easily spooked, fighting the bit every step of the way, and she became very hard to stop. She was rushing and pacing all the time. We had several incidents where she bolted, and we ended up in very dangerous situations.

By the time she was five, my parents had built a simple little arena covered in wood chips for me to ride. I thought that in order to solve my issues with Mazirah, I should give her some schooling, but even in that arena, she was tense, rushing and fighting the bit. When cantering, we even fell a few times, so I grew nervous, and very soon I just didn't canter anymore. I did everything I could to set up the sessions well, to be patient to stay calm. But every once in a while, I lost my temper and took it out on Mazirah.

I was devastated. My dream was breaking. Now she had no reason at all to want to be with me. And she confirmed that. Each time she saw me coming, wearing my riding boots, she would just walk away. It took me thirty minutes to catch her in the field. The frustration I felt was suffocating. I just wanted to hide from myself.

And then Mazirah's first foal, Mayana, was born. I clearly remember the night of Mayana's birth. I woke up because I was dreaming about Mazirah. I got up, went into the barn in my pyjamas, and there the foal was, just born. I remember watching her take her first wobbly steps, searching for the milk bar. And I swore to myself I wouldn't create the same relationship with her as I had with her mother. I made a decision: *I will get help and do everything necessary to create a fulfilling and lasting relationship we both enjoy.* I made the decision to make her dignity and happiness my priority, because if she was happy in our relationship, I would be happy too.

Reaching my horse's heart

I went on a journey of 100 percent commitment to learn the secrets about how to reach a horse's heart. After finishing my professional education in Equine Reproduction, Training and Services, I decided my learning was far from done. As I still had no money for courses and lessons, I became a working student of Berni Zambail for six months.

This experience saved my dream. I learned many secrets about horses, about what my horse really needs and how to explain everything to Mazirah. I learned what it takes to gain my horse's confidence and build rapport, and how to establish the connection I always dreamt of having.

I learned to understand myself and to develop the leader inside of me. I learned to deeply understand my horse's nature and how she perceives the world without projecting any human thoughts onto her. And I learned to understand the process, the order of tasks, what it takes to educate a horse step by step to become a reliable and happy partner. Soon, Mazirah was not running off anymore, but greeting me at the gate. This was the best feedback I could get from her, confirming that I was on the right track.

The years went by, and I kept learning, reading, and studying. I managed to make my passion my everyday job at the stables of Marie Claire de Selliers in the heart of France. I began to start horses for other people, or to help them when they experienced some trouble with their horses. I met so many people, who just like me, had a broken dream. It became my passion to help horses understand their owners and help the owners to understand their horses better. I worked with horses and riders from all kind of disciplines: leisure riders who just wanted to enjoy trail rides; Western riders who loved reining and going on trail competitions; jumping riders whose horses didn't load into the trailer, which made going to competitions impossible; dressage riders whose horses refused to enter the competition ring; people with experience in natural horsemanship and groundwork; and people who had no experience at all. My goal has always been to bring understanding and peace into horse-human relationships.

I figured out that it really isn't about what task to do when, or what method is right or wrong, or what technique or tools you use. Rather, what really counts is to understand the principles of good horsemanship and to act out of love for the horse.

Success starts with you

It really is about learning to understand yourself, becoming aware of your dreams and motivations, developing the leader inside yourself, and adopting a mindset based on self-awareness. It's about learning to deeply understand the nature of the horse, how horses learn, think and perceive the world around them. It's about understanding the process of educating a horse and creating with awareness the relationship we wish to have. This book aims to empower YOU by learning to understand yourself, your horse and the process so that you can make independent decisions of what works and what doesn't work for your unique horse and your personal goals.

I could give you a fish, but you would benefit much more if I would teach you to fish. By understanding the principles, you will be able to decide for yourself and become independent of any horse training method out there. This book will demystify the horse and what it takes to achieve extraordinary results.

Whenever I go to the field to my horse Mayana, the best days are those when she answers my call with a soft nicker and comes from far away to meet me. This simple thing, her wanting to spend time with me, fills my heart with happiness. It is a glimpse of the dream come true.

In summer, when the fields are harvested, I often go with Mayana for long, fast rides over the open fields, her wearing nothing but a neck rope. The power, the speed, the flying mane, the dust of the hooves, just us flying towards the sunset being untamed and wild: this makes me feel free and connected to the pure elements of life, the power, exuberance, beauty, freedom!

I have kept my promise to myself: to create a happy horse and to have a fulfilling relationship for both of us with Mayana. Now, I want to share with you how you can let this dream of a fulfilling and happy relationship with your youngster come alive.

How to use this book

To get the most out of this book I created a workbook for you. You can download it here: https://www.understandingisthekey.com/workbook

Every chapter ends with a little exercise to help you gain a deeper understanding about the elements of your horse dream and what it takes to reach it. Complete the exercises right away, after each chapter when the content is still fresh in your mind. Later you can use the book as your go-to resource when you hit a roadblock, have some questions, or want to plan out a new training chapter with your horse.

I like to keep books like this on my bedside table. I will read a few random paragraphs every evening. This keeps my mind inspired.

Let's get started!

Part 1:

Understand Yourself

MY DREAM
LEADERSHIP
RESOURCES
MINDSET

This first part of the book is all about setting YOU up for success. I have seen so many human/horse couples end in disaster, and the one main reason is that the owners have been running blindly behind their dream. Having a dream is important; it gives you power. By gaining full awareness about it, you can use its power in a good way to prevent it from turning into a nightmare.

What does it take from your side to make this dream come true? Get real, get honest, and let's talk facts about your goals, your motivations and about what resources you need to take into consideration. Discover what I call the "Power Mindset" and how you can uncover the leader within yourself your horse wants and needs.

Before you try to understand your horse, you need to learn to understand yourself. Your horse will reflect not just what you present to the outside, but how you feel inside, so horse training begins with you.

The Dream within Us

hy do you have a horse? What a question to start a horse book! Of course, it's because you love them! Me too. But why exactly do we love them? Why are we ready to invest so much money and time into this passion of ours? Why are we ready to accept all kind of inconveniences for our horse? This is a very important question, and its answer will give you the energy to push through difficulties.

It's a fact that "horse people" are a different kind of people. People may think we are kinda crazy with straw in our car and mud on our boots. They stare at us while we're out shopping in our dirty riding breeches with our helmet-hair or our hair all fluffed up from wind and rain. Our partners complain that we spend more time with the horse than with them. We are constantly broke because we spend every spare penny on our horse. We go out and scoop poop in the most hostile conditions and get all stinky. Our horse eats healthier than we do and his stable is cleaner than our house! We get bucked off, stepped on, and dragged around, and still our horses are the most precious things to us.

I became a crazy horse-dream chaser the first day I sat on a pony. I am exactly the way described above, yet I must admit I couldn't give a real answer to this question until I was forced to give it some serious thought. In summer 2017, I had a bad fall from Mayana during a training for our next endurance ride. I suffered a severe cranial trauma and lost my memory for quite some time. For several weeks, I didn't even feel drawn to my horses anymore. It felt as if a part of myself had vanished. So, there I was, a horse-crazy woman whose life were her horses and who didn't feel it anymore. Could I fall in love with horses again in the same way?

Every day my husband took me to visit my horses, especially my one-month-old foal, Maserati. I had forgotten that my favorite mare had a foal! It took two months until I felt "it" again. But finally, my love returned, with much more clarity.

I love them for how they are, their beauty, their smell, the way they make me feel I am home. For the friendship they can give, the non-judgmental feedback, their honesty. I want to spend my days with them, outside in nature with the smell of hay, the wind in my hair, the sun in my face (and the rain, too). Their company makes me feel grounded instantly. I love to feel their soft noses in my neck, smell their breath, and bury my face in their mane. Horse smell is the best perfume ever. I want to feel the power and freedom of thundering hooves, galloping over open fields, carrying me away from everyday obligations and worries and giving me a moment of freedom, suspended in time.

With my horse, I feel the connection to another soul. We understand each other's thoughts; silent communication made possible through energy exchange. The harmony and peace and quiet joy I feel when I am with one of my horses playing at liberty makes me forget everything else in my life. It recharges my batteries, refreshes my soul. Horses are my oxygen.

I remember a day - dream I had when I was just six years old and hadn't even been in contact with horses yet. In the dream, I am lying on my pony's back. It is a warm and sunny day. The birds are singing. There is a soft, warm breeze gently stroking my cheeks. We are alone, just us, happy and peaceful. She is grazing quietly, and I can feel the warmth of her back, the softness of her mane, and I can hear how she is munching the grass. I feel at home, happy, and free. When I was older, I dreamt about us being true friends, and she would come running whenever she saw me coming. Of course, I wouldn't need any halter, bridle or saddle to ride her! And yes, it was clearly a she; today I own four mares, and I am as close to living the dream as I've ever been. When I play with Mayana, our play becomes a dance where both of us know every single move and I forget time and space. When in summer the fields are harvested, I can go with Mayana for long and fast rides over the open fields, her wearing just a rope around her neck.

I am pretty sure you too had a similar horse dream when you were little. Maybe your dream was to canter on the beach, that your horse would understand you without words, that you are the only one who was able to ride the difficult horse, that your horse would love to be with you and wait for you every day at the gate. Maybe you were inspired by a TV series like *Black Beauty* and carried that dream of having a horse be your closest friend within you since then.

Maybe you weren't born into a horse family, yet like me, had an innate fascination somewhere in your DNA, wanting to touch every horse you see. When you were sitting in the back of the car, you were imagining riding a white pony alongside the car, taking bold jumps over the street signs on the side of the road. Being free and wild, faster than anyone!

At this point, maybe you are asking yourself why I am writing about this at length. The reason is simple: This dream, this longing, is what drives everything we do with horses—consciously or unconsciously, good and bad. It also motivates us to take the first step towards a goal, it keeps us going and pursuing through all difficulties.

Because of this dream, you went on one of the most exciting adventures in a horse owner's life: bringing up a young horse from scratch.

Why choose a young horse?

Maybe our dream entails choosing a young horse with all its unique challenges. Why would we do this?

Young horses have a special energy. They are so pure, happy, curious, innocent and sparkling. They are so full of life. The ways they explore the world, experience things and learn are so wonderful to witness. With each of my young horses, I experience the same pure joy of life when being with them. They are invigorating and refreshing to the soul.

There are many reasons why we decide to buy a young horse. Three of my horses I own right now were either born in my arms or I bought as a weanling. My other two mares I bought both green and unstarted at age three and eight respectively. I love to develop my horses, to create a trusting relationship, and I love to see them evolve and grow. I have total control over everything they learn and experience, and I also know where the occasional bad habits come from. They are all my responsibility and my pleasure. They are, in a sense, my creations.

But wouldn't it save us some hassle to buy an already educated, more experienced horse? We put up with waiting many years until we can ride our horse, we spend a lot of money in raising our little friend, and we have so many little worries until he is fully grown. And yet we have many good reasons why we would buy a young, green horse.

We want to establish a special relationship

The relationship can grow slowly over the years. There is no pressure of performance. No pressure that things have to happen now and not only in a few weeks. We can get to know each other inside out at our pace. We can start right at the beginning to create the relationship we dream of.

The relationships I have with my two horses who were born at home are different from the relationships I have with my horses I bought later in their lives. Somehow, the level of mutual trust is more distinct. Because I have known them since the very beginning, I know how they will react to everything in almost every situation. And they, in return, learned that I am there for them when they feel worried. We are family.

We want to be in control of our horse's education

Maybe you have already owned a horse with serious bad habits. Some habits can be changed, but it takes a lot more time to correct behavior than teaching good habits right from the beginning. The first four years in a horse's life are crucial in his development. This is the time when the "software" is installed. Everything a horse learns during this age and every experience he has will be deeply embedded. It is normal to want to be in control of you horse's education if you have already had a bad experience. To be in charge of what, when and how your horse learns is a nice challenge and a big responsibility.

I see my young horses like a fresh canvas; I can paint whatever I like. Each moment I spend with them, I do a stroke with my brush. If I have a plan and I stick with it over several years, I will have a wonderful painting I can enjoy every single time I look at it. However, if I don't pay attention, I might make an ugly spot, but at least I know which paint I need to undo the mistake.

We want our horse to grow up in a good environment

Many health and lameness issues in horses are related to poor living conditions and shortages of minerals in early years. A lot of problems can be avoided when we pay close attention to how our youngster grows up. Living outside in a herd ensures that muscles, tendons, joints and bones get the stimulation needed to develop to their full strength. In addition to that, growing horses need to receive adequate and balanced levels of minerals and vitamins for healthy development and growth.

We want to limit expense

Horses are more expensive to buy the older and more educated they are. When I bought my horse Tara, I was actually looking for a four- to seven-year-old already ridden Shagya-Arabian mare. I had been looking for a while, but my dream mare was simply not available in my budget and at that moment. That's why I decided to buy Tara when she was just five months old. I knew that she would turn into my dream mare once she reached adult age, but she was three times less expensive than an adult. Of course we have to take all the expenses into account that will follow during the next years.

We want to keep a foal from our favorite mare

Maybe you want to keep something of your favorite horse with you forever. This is an absolutely beautiful experience. I was blessed to live this two times with Mazirah and her two foals, Mayana and Maserati.

Both times I was there when she was giving birth and witnessed the foals' first wobbly attempts to stand up. The first time they said hello to me and curiously explored me with their little noses was the moment I absolutely fell in love with them. To experience their trust when they rested their heads in my lap to take a nap was simply magical. The relationship I have to these two horses is very different than to any other horse.

We want to enjoy seeing our horse grow up

To experience the whole process of growing up and maturing can be very satisfying. They change every day and have new ideas every day as they develop. There will be many ups and downs. The end goal is far away; it will take years to reach it. But it's about the beauty of the journey towards that goal. That's why it is so important to know exactly where you want to go. It helps to have a mental picture of how you would like your dream horse to turn out in the end. We have the chance to build and create it step by step and enjoy the process on the way.

But there is also a danger to this passion of ours. This dream can control us on a subconscious level and drive us to make decisions without taking the facts of our life into consideration. And then this dream can turn very quickly into a nightmare.

When our horse dreams become nightmares

One summer, a girl came to me to get some help with her horse. She brought a beautiful Palomino mare, six years old. The mare was absolutely stunning with a tall, perfect body and fantastic movement. She was super-expressive and extroverted. You just had to stop and look. The girl had acquired the horse young and wanted to grow together with her. A friend had helped to start the mare, and the horse lived with an old pony at the girl's home.

The girl had no arena and only little time, as she was still going to school. Her only possibility to ride her was on trail rides. But the mare became increasingly spooky and difficult out on the trail, and the girl got more and more afraid of her horse.

Then the mare had an accident in the trailer, which caused the mare to become almost impossible to handle even in everyday life. She would act up, rear and kick whenever she didn't understand, or thought that there was something scary. And because the girl was so terrified of her by now, she wasn't able to give her the leadership she needed in those moments.

So, there she was, owning the horse of her dreams with amazing potential, but one that was way too spirited for her abilities, knowledge and confidence. She didn't even dare to lead her horse the 100 meters from the barn to the pasture.

We made a lot of progress on the ground during the ten days she spent with me. The mare regained trust and respect and was again easy to handle in everyday life. But both the horse and the girl were far from ready to ride. The girl hadn't taken into consideration how much time and discipline it takes to develop a horse with this high level of spirit into a reliable partner.

This girl had acted out of impulse; driven by an unconscious dream without taking into consideration the resources she had available to actually make her dream a reality.

Use your dream as motivation

This dream of yours deserves to work out, to be fulfilled. Wouldn't it be a pity to invest so much time, money, effort and hard work for it to end in a disaster? It is sad and heartbreaking. All this frustration isn't necessary, and you can avoid it. Dreams have an incredible power. They drive us to new heights, motivate us to grow, and to do things we would have never thought possible. The dream can give you superpowers … but it can also lead us to some very stupid decisions. You don't have to go down the bumpy road if you use the power of your dream the right way. It's up to you to use the power of the dream for your advantage and find it fulfilled, or to allow it to control you and lead you to frustration and pain.

I would be foolish to encourage you with flowery words to follow the calling of your dreams and leap without looking. I know where it leads if you don't add several drops of reason and good common sense to the dream.

If you want to tap into the power of the dream, you need to get crystal clear about what drives you. What is your motivation and where do you want to go? What do you want to achieve? This clarity will give you the ability, motivation and discipline to take controlled and sensible decisions to make your dream become reality.

To fulfill this dream is absolutely worth all the struggle, pain and effort. But you should do everything you can in your power to keep the pain as low as possible and the chances to succeed as high as possible.

Exercise:
So, what's your dream?

Turn to chapter 1 in the workbook for some reflection on your dream. Haven't got the workbook yet? Download it here: https://www.understandingisthekey.com/workbook

If you prefer, you can reflect using your own journal and answer the following questions:

What was your childhood dream about horses?

What attracts you so magically?

When do you feel the happiest when being with horses?

What do horses give you emotionally?

How does it make you feel if your horse greets you?

What is your dream that you want to achieve with your horse? Where do you want this journey to take you?

What is your WHY?

Get it out of the dark and become aware, so it won't control you on a subconscious level. Let your answers be your fuel.

Resources You Need

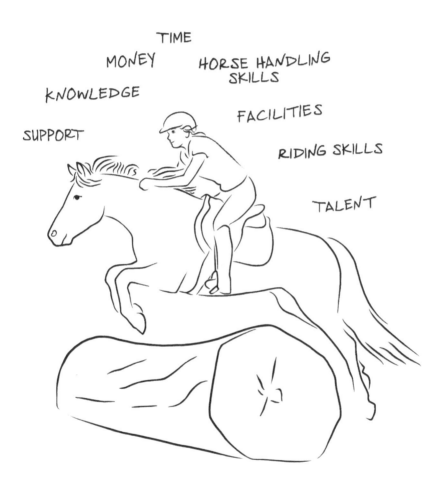

TIME

MONEY   HORSE HANDLING SKILLS

KNOWLEDGE

FACILITIES

SUPPORT

RIDING SKILLS

TALENT

Do you know those fantastic little French chocolate cakes called "Moelleux au Chocolat"? They're crispy on the outside with a velvety hot liquid chocolate center. If you want to bake the Moelleux au Chocolat just right, you need very specific ingredients. Similarly, getting your horse dream just right requires certain resources in exact amounts. Too little or too much of one ingredient, neither the cake nor the horse will turn out the way you had imagined.

Imagine you want to make the famous Moelleux au Chocolat. You need five eggs, but you only have three. This leaves you with four choices. You could go to neighbor and ask him/her to help you out, you could downsize the cake, you could go shopping for more eggs, or you will have to accept that the cake will be odd.

Same is true with your horse dream. To reach your ideal destination, you need to make sure that you have certain resources available. Too little of one resource and the end result might not fit your hoped-for outcome. Luckily, broken dreams and dashed hopes can be mended (as opposed to a screwed up cake) as long as you're willing to be honest with yourself and seek alternative solutions to the ones you may be using.

To put it simply, it is not enough to have a dream and to keep it alive. Because I want to set you up for success with this book, part of the necessary work is to do a painfully honest reality check with yourself.

Be willing to ask for help

A few years back, a lady (let's call her Jan) asked if I could board the weanling filly she had bought. She told me that with buying the filly, she fulfilled a childhood dream of owning a black Spanish horse with a long mane and proud yet gentle temperament. She found a breeder who offered to reserve the foals already in utero. The horses were absolutely magnificent; both parents were black. So, the lady jumped at the offer. It was Jan's first time owning a horse, and she didn't have much experience with horses in general beyond some classical riding lessons at a local club.

The filly arrived at our place. She settled in well in the new herd. She grew a lot, both physically and mentally. And, typically for her breed, she was bold, sensitive, and had very quick reflexes, which are necessary for bullfighting.

I fed and handled the filly for everyday tasks. I was attentive to setting boundaries and advised Jan to do the same. But the lady disregarded the advice, fed treats to the filly, and didn't care if the filly respected the most basic rules of being polite. She was worried that the filly wouldn't like her if she set limits. Soon, the filly became more and more cocky and dominant. But Jan refused offers for lessons or help with educating the filly beyond the basic tasks.

Finally, when the filly was a year old and had grown taller than her owner, Jan finally asked me for help. She had decided to take the filly home so it could live with one other gelding she had impulsively bought. The purchase of the gelding was initially a good plan. The idea was that she would have an older, well-educated horse to ride and get more experience from until her filly was ready to ride.

But she chose the wrong gelding. He too was a Spanish horse with lots of blood and quick reflexes. He was castrated very late and wasn't used to living with other horses. Because Jan wasn't a good rider, she constantly disturbed the horse by being off balance and gripping onto the reins to ease her fear. This caused the usually very gentle horse to become afraid and difficult to ride.

I had just two short weeks to teach the filly all the essential skills: to lead properly, to be alone with confidence, to give the feet, to trailer load, to stand tied and, most importantly, to respect boundaries and behave politely towards people. The filly learned with the speed of light; she was simply amazing.

Both horses then went to live at Jan's place. I got news occasionally, none of it very good. The gelding started to mount the little filly whenever she was in heat; the filly quickly fell back into her dominant behavior towards people, especially towards Jan's two sons; the two horses developed a very strong bond, so it was soon impossible to take one out of the pasture alone; they would act up, rear, run, and break the fences. The filly even noticed that the electricity in the fence wasn't on all the time and started to escape quite often! Jan didn't have an arena or round pen, so her only option was a trail ride … this was impossible for obvious reasons.

And still Jan wasn't willing to ask for help. She had two beautiful horses in her field of which she was so afraid that she wasn't able to ride. She didn't have the finances to invest in the proper education of herself and her horses, so she wasn't able to do anything with her horses except admire them and scoop their poop. Jan had acted out of impulse, driven by an unconscious dream, without taking into considerations the resources she had available to her to make it work.

Success will depend upon your resources

Unfortunately, I see people like Jan quite often. And this is sad to watch. Too many horse owners buy themselves a horse in the category of a Ferrari but only have the driving license for a VW Polo.

You can avoid this nightmare by getting fully aware of your resources available to you. Do yourself and your horse the favor of being brutally honest with yourself, not only about your skills as a rider but also when it comes to handling horses. Evaluate how much time, effort, and money are you able and willing to invest into this adventure.

Let's look at the necessary resources.

Horse handling and riding skills

How good are you handling horses? Do you have experience with groundwork? With a young horse, you will naturally need to do a lot of work on the ground before you can ride him later.

How good a rider are you? How confident are you? Are you experienced riding different horses? How skilled are you when riding through delicate situations? How good is your seat?

If you aren't experienced and still lack skills in any of these areas, you can always learn and improve. Use the time your horse is growing up to ride other horses to develop your skill levels. So that you are ready when it's time to start riding your youngster, practice groundwork with an older horse and take lessons.

Knowledge

How much do you know about general horse keeping, horse health, proper tack fit, equine learning, horsemanship, and riding? Unfortunately, we never know what we don't know. Being with horses means never-ending learning. Fortunately, this is a resource that is very easy to find, and just reading this book means you are already doing it.

The more you know in theory, the more you can use in practice in real-life situations with your horse. If you don't know much yet, do everything you can to fill up on knowledge in every area of horsemanship.

Talent

I don't want to hurt anybody's feelings here, but just as not everybody is a talented pianist, not everybody is a talented rider. But there is good news: patient and persistent work still lead to great ability. I am not at all talented when it comes to jumping. I just don't like it, and can't get the feel for it. I worked a lot on it, I improved a lot, but what I can do now is the fruit of hard work and not innate talent. Naturally, I won't buy myself a horse whose main talent is jumping because I wouldn't be able to tap into his full potential and wouldn't be able to use the horse for what I truly love doing.

Does your natural talent fit the horse? Does the horse's talents match your goal?

Time

It takes a lot of time to train a young horse from scratch. Don't expect miracles if you aren't able to put in a certain amount of time. However, it is okay if you can't spend time on your horse's education for a few weeks. What I like to do, and advise horse owners to do, is plan ahead for the most important building blocks of your horse's education. Take the summer holidays, or a long weekend to really focus on a certain topic with your horse. You will make faster progress if you have a solid plan and strong focus for a short, intense period of time, than if you do only one session of random tasks every week.

Different types of horses require different amount of time. Hot and spirited horses don't tend to do so well if you take them out only once or twice a week. On the other hand, laid-back breeds don't mind doing something occasionally. If you can invest a lot of time, good for you: you will be able to make amazing progress.

And if you really can't put in the necessary time for your horse's most important foundational training, ask a trainer to do it for you.

Money

We all know horses are an expensive hobby. They literally turn our money into crap! Jan, the lady with the black Spanish mare, didn't have the finances to invest in her own education or her horse's, so the money she spent on buying and maintaining the horses was somehow wasted.

If you already have the skill and knowledge, having limited finances isn't such a big deal because you are able to educate and take proper care of your horse on your own. But if you lack experience, skill, time, or knowledge, you need to be willing to invest money to compensate for that.

There was a time I wasn't able to afford even a weekend course. Not even proper equipment. I rode bareback for years in the beginning, and I only had one bridle, which I used on five different ponies. I bought tons of educational books with the little money I had. (Somehow, I knew that knowledge was the one most important key that would enable me to reach my goal.) Then I exchanged work for lessons so I had access to good trainers and the education I needed to reach my goals. I'm proof that there are ways to get around having little money.

Facilities

Where can you train your horse? Especially with a young horse, you need some sort of arena or at least round pen that you can train safely and effectively. Having no arena or round pen when you have a young horse will limit and slow your progress.

Unless you are very experienced on trail rides, you should have someone with an experienced horse come with you when going out with a young horse. But more often than not, young horses will not be confident out alone. Therefore, it will be much easier if the horse can learn the basics at home in a safe arena first.

If you don't have a pen or arena, maybe you can go to a neighbor's stable, or fence off a level part of your pasture.

Support

Bringing on a young horse from scratch is a huge task. Unless you are very experienced with horses, you will need support at some point. Once we start to learn from others, we realize how blind we have been.

Support may come in many different forms. If you are lucky, you have a trainer you trust nearby to take regular lessons with. An experienced friend can help a lot, even if it is just to accompany you on trail rides with his calm horse. Online courses and video coaching can be a good solution if you live far away from any trainer you can trust.

A pair of experienced eyes will be able to see issues you cannot. That person can point you in the right direction and give you important tips to untangle a knot you may have been tied up in for a while. I know it myself: there are certain things we just don't see ourselves because we have gotten so hung up on it. Don't hesitate to ask for support. Don't stay stuck or walking the wrong way too long, just ask for help. For your horse's sake!

Now that you have done the honest self-evaluation of the external resources you have, you have these options for taking action:

1. Downsize the goal and dream to fit your resources
2. Upgrade your resources and invest into your own and your horse's education
3. If everything fits perfectly, you are ready to go!

Attitude is critical

In addition to the practical resources you will need, there are certain traits you need to succeed.

Willingness to grow

Don't stay in your current situation if it doesn't fit; instead, change and grow. It's no good searching the internet for some miracle method or solution that promises to fix your horse instantly. This is just not how this works! If you can't put in the time, have no discipline, can't find the money, or aren't willing to up your knowledge and skills, you shouldn't be surprised that it is not working out.

Learning means stepping out of your comfort zone. Growth is uncomfortable. In a way, it's admitting that we have been wrong, and that's why we so often find ourselves staying in our pit of hopelessness. Every single time, we must make a conscious decision to take the next step towards our dream.

But when we can see the fruits of all our hard work and efforts, it feels great. When we realize how much we have grown and improved, we feel proud of ourselves. And this is when the power of the dream comes back in play, and you are motivated to put in the effort, to keep pushing, to outgrow yourself, and rise out of the pit of despair and defeat.

Positive mindset

Maybe there is another reason that might be holding you back: you don't believe enough in yourself. It is way easier to sink into a pit of feeling sorry and hopeless, than to step out of it and take the first step to action. Every single human is born with the innate ability to create things. Just have a look in history. People had an idea, and when they started to act on that dream, they created empires, invented incredible gadgets, and made enduring art. It is the power of our minds and our passion that leads us to action and makes the impossible possible.

You are no different! You too have that ability to create and bring your dream to life! It might be hard sometimes, and it will take discipline and effort, but it is possible. You are stronger than you think you are. You can achieve more than you think you can. You can grow to fit the size of your dream! My resources didn't fit my horse or my dream when I started out. Heart and desire, paired with some reason and thought, made up for not having much money, knowledge facilities and talent.

How to choose the right horse

(If you already have your horse, you may skip this section!)

There is one more resource that deserves a closer look: choosing the right horse. You deserve to have the horse of your dreams, the horse that really fits you. You wouldn't marry someone you didn't really love to be with in the long run, would you?

When buying a young horse, it is oftentimes a decision of the heart. If you want to make your dream a success, it helps to sit down and think about what kind of horse would suit you to add a few drops of reason to your heart decision.

Where do you want to go? What discipline would you like to do with your horse?

Would you like to do some kind of action-loaded discipline such as show jumping or endurance? Or do you simply want to enjoy trail rides and the occasional ride in an arena? Would you like to work cows, race barrels or do some dressage shows? Answers to these questions may affect what type of horse you choose.

Breeds

Certain breeds have certain traits. Of course, there is always the exception to be found, but if you are a timid rider who wants to enjoy quiet trail rides, don't buy an Arabian, Thoroughbred, or a Spanish horse. Yes, they are beautiful to look at, but they also have lots of speed and fast reactions. You would probably be much happier with a more laid-back breed, such as a Haflinger or an Irish Cob.

It follows then that if you love action-loaded disciplines and speed, you will love a high-spirited Arabian, thoroughbred, or a well-bred warmblood. These horses also require a higher level of skill and demand more of your time.

How much time are you able to invest will be an important factor in your decision. High-spirited horses will need more hours per week of physical activity and a very regular training schedule to be at their best. Laid-back breeds in the contrary won't mind hanging out in the field for longer periods.

Mare, gelding or stallion?

First of all, if you are not highly experienced and have no breeding purposes, don't buy a stallion! He will be frustrated and you will be frustrated. A good stallion will make a fantastic gelding.

If you take a mare or a gelding, it is about preference. Geldings tend to have a very steady temperament, as they have no hormonal cycle that influences mood. Geldings tend to be steady and reliable in their everyday performance.

I love mares. Just like women, they have clear opinions and a strong sense of dignity and fairness! Once you have established a relationship with them, they put lots of effort for you and are very loving. But it is true that when they are in season, they can be a bit moody at times.

Different personalities

Just like people, horses have different personalities. Every horse is different, but in general we can divide them into four main types:

1. Introverted
2. Extroverted
3. Courageous and dominant
4. Fearful and timid

I will explain in detail all four personalities in Chapter 7 and which characters fit best with which type of rider. In short, though, an extroverted and bold rider wouldn't be a wonderful match for an introverted or fearful horse. He would either overwhelm the horse or find the horse boring. Similarly, an introverted and fearful person may become very afraid of an extroverted horse and will not be able to give the leadership necessary to that horse.

You can always influence a horse with good education, but you can't change the innate character. So, choose wisely and add some reason to you heart decision. Maybe your horse will be a little less pretty and fancy, but you will be much less frustrated and a lot happier in the long run.

When I bought Mazirah as a three-year-old, I didn't have much experience yet. I only had a vague picture of the horse I wanted to buy. I didn't think well about whether she would match my own personality or if she would fit my goals. From the first second I saw her, and she looked at me, I knew it had to be her. It was a complete heart decision. The first five years together were very difficult. She was green, hot and sensitive, and I didn't have the skill and knowledge required to properly educate a horse like her. I was angry and frustrated way too often, she was scared and felt lost so many times. For sure, we were not a match made in heaven. Today, I can say, that thanks to her (and some very knowledgeable mentors), our relationship is strong. But if you aren't young, athletic and crazy and don't have the ambition and drive to go through trouble like this, I suggest you do the best you can to avoid it.

Exercise:
Visualize your horse
and your resources

Head over to chapter 2 in the workbook. There, you'll find guides for reflecting on your dream horse and evaluating your resources. If you haven't downloaded the workbook yet, you can get it here: https://www.understandingisthekey.com/workbook

Or, take out your journal and make two lists. First, write down how you would like your dream horse to be. What does the horse look like? What personality will he/she have? What would you like to do with him/her later (trail rides, dressage, liberty, show jumping, eventing,endurance)?

In the second list, write down the resources you have right now available to you: your level of skill handling horses on the ground and as a rider, level of confidence and courage, the time you can spend, the financial investment you are able to make, the knowledge you have and your own personality.

Now compare the two. You will quickly see where your picture of your dream horse fits you and where you need to adjust or work on.

A New Perspective
on Leadership

L eadership is a big word in horse world. Every horse person has heard the sentence: "You have to become a better leader for your horse." Yes, I know. But how? What does that actually mean? How can I become the leader my horse needs and, most importantly, appreciates?

When it comes to leadership, the horse world divides into two main camps. One says, "You need to show him who is boss and get his feet moving into your direction!" The other says, "You are equals, I won't make my horse do anything he doesn't want to do. He can choose."

At one time, I found myself going from one camp to the other, trying out different techniques. Eventually, I realized that the truth lies in the middle ground between the two camps. And that middle ground has a lot to do with you, personally.

There is so much talk about "harmony training," "liberty training," "freedom training" and more. Every one of these trainers and methods seems to promise the ultimate relationship without designating a leader in the relationship, advising you to set limits when needed. They all seem to promise that they have a miracle method. But these methods won't work for everyone, especially if you simply don't have the time and experience needed to make them work. I believe that we are drawn so strongly towards these methods because of a fundamental misunderstanding about what leadership truly means.

Horses ask us to step up and be a strong person. This can feel uncomfortable to some. We hope, that by just being "nice" and "gentle" to the horse, one day he will love us so much that he will do anything for us. I am not a person who likes to beat around the bush—there has been too much of that when it comes to this topic. I believe we need to get a whole new understanding of leadership and how to uncover the natural leader within us.

Being nice isn't enough

Of course, we should be nice to our horse. But what is "nice"? To me, being nice to a horse means giving him boundaries he can rely on. For the owner, this means stepping up, being a strong person, knowing what you want, and asking for it. Being clear will give the horse peace of mind: no gray area, no "maybes," and no "would you mind if … and not leaving your horse in doubt about what you want him to do."

Does that mean being rude to the horse? Not at all. Does it mean that we must dominate our horse? Not at all. It means being responsible, keeping the big picture in mind, and leading.

A good leader can be both firm and certain, as well as listening and empathic. Many women in particular have no problem with the listening and supportive sides of leadership. I meet many women of all ages who find it very difficult though to uncover the firm and certain side in themselves (including myself). In the critical moments, so many doubts and guilty/inadequate feelings surface and undermine leadership. Why is it so hard to show presence, to act with determination, and to say NO? Why is it so hard to assert what we want without feeling bad?

Fact is, if you want to have a safe and successful relationship with your horse, you need to guide and lead your horse in a way he can understand. It is absolutely essential that our horses have a certain amount of obedience and respect so that we can be safe.

You are the one with the overview in this relationship. You are the one who can evaluate situations. Horses can't think that way, so you have to be the leader, the decision-maker in order to keep both of you safe. You can learn to do that through understanding what kind of leadership a horse needs, and by giving your own voice and person more value, at least the same value as you give your horse's needs.

Boss horses and lead horses: What nature can teach us

Is it possible to implement nature's model in our training? Let's look at how boss horses differ from lead horses.

The boss horse

In my herd of mares, where we integrate weanlings, there is an older mare called Bahia who is clearly the boss mare. When she comes, every other horse moves without questioning. She drinks first, and the others don't dare join her at the hay bale without asking permission at least three times. She is not being aggressive in any way, although I saw her kick and bite with great assertiveness in her younger years when she found it necessary to get her point across. Still now, whenever she shows her limits to one of the foals, she uses very assertive body language in clearly distinguishable phases. I also observed Bahia clear out eventual fights between other horses. In this herd, she ensures that the rules of living together are kept. She is responsible for peace and safety.

The lead horse

When I had to wean my foal, Maserati, off his mother, Mazirah, I moved her to another herd. She didn't know any of the other horses, but quickly became friends with my other mare, Salimah. With the three other horses of the herd, Mazirah stayed distant and actually got pushed around by them and ended up being fourth out of five in the pecking order. Over time, though, whenever Mazirah started to walk somewhere, she was not only followed by her new friend Salimah but also higher ranking horses. Mazirah, being a very active horse, began bringing new life into this herd. Even the two older horses, who were always standing at their hay rack eating and growing their bellies, came to new life. They would walk around a lot more, following Mazirah and her activities. Mazirah was the one who would lead the whole herd from one place to another. Somehow everyone trusted her judgment that it was safe to go to certain places.

At Haras Naturel du Plessis, the place I worked in France, we had four different herds. Through the years, I constantly observed the boss and lead dynamics I just described. In every herd, I was able to observe the same thing: one horse who is the boss, but not necessarily the leader, and another horse that oftentimes initiates activity and movement whom even the more bossy one will follow.

I have read it and heard it myself many times—if you want to be your horse's respected leader, you have to be able to control his feet. If you are able to control your horse's feet in speed and direction, he will decide that you are the higher-ranking horse and choose to trust and follow you. This idea is based on the belief that there is one mare in the herd who is the boss who decides where to go, when to go for a drink, and when to run from danger. By establishing her leadership over every other member of the herd (controlling their feet), she ensures the safety of the whole herd.

Is the nature model outdated?

The German scientist Konstanze Krüger, and also new French studies from Marie Bourjade, call into question the whole concept of a "lead mare" making most decisions in a herd.[1,2]

The studies show some evidence of consensus in decision-making. Movement within the herd, at least, can involve any member of the group initiating the activity by simply departing. Higher ranking horses though were followed more often by other horses than lower ranking horses. There doesn't seem to be a lead mare in the sense of one horse which makes all the decisions for the group, but the studies found that the hierarchy was strong within the herds, though everyday decisions were not necessarily done by the boss.

This also leads to the idea that being the "boss" of your horse doesn't necessarily mean that you would automatically be the leader your horse would choose to follow.

But they also found that, if in a herd there was a strong female boss mare, that the herd was more peaceful and had less fights between each other.

This leads to the conclusion that if you want to be safe with your horse, you need to show a presence and insist on a certain level of obedience in daily interaction. Your horse will be calmer, more confident and, therefore, safer. But you need to develop a few more qualities so that the horse also chooses to follow you because, in nature, horses are free to choose whether they want to follow or not. I would like my horses to choose to follow me.

Key factors of great leadership

There seem to be two completely different types of leadership. Which one should we follow and apply to our horses? Maybe neither of them is entirely applicable to the interspecies relationship we have with our horse. You are just not a horse!

If we behaved only like the horse who initiates movement, we could never be sure that our horse would listen to us when it really matters. However, if we only act like the bossy horse, we might have obedience, but the horse might not want to spend time with us.

It is time that we develop a whole new perspective about leadership, perhaps using some parts of both models: Be the lead but sometimes also the boss. Let's look at what makes good leadership.

A good leader is self-aware

We must act with open eyes. We need to develop a high level of self-awareness. This applies to all aspects: what we think, what we feel, and what our body does. We need to become conscious about the why, how, and what of our goals, motivations, feelings, and actions. Most people spend most of their time being unaware of any of these.

This requires constant work and attention. There will be moments when we notice that we have been acting completely unaware, and these moments of realization are so often perceived as defeat. However, in fact, these moments are ones of victory because you are back to awareness!

Being aware means to create on purpose, with full knowledge. This will help us to become more and more sure of ourselves and we will be able to be authentic and real towards our horses.

Empathy is crucial

Meet your horse with an open heart. Love and understanding goes a long way with humans and also with horses. Any action should be motivated from empathy and love for the horse.

We have to see the world from the horse's point of view in order to understand the reactions we don't like so much in our horse. Every horse needs something different to be able to connect to us: some need us to speak more quietly and give them more room, while some horses, especially extroverted ones with a big personality, ask us to show more presence and to speak up so that they can recognize us as an equal being. We have to take care for our horse's emotional, physical, and mental well-being and make sure that they are safe from danger, healthy, and sound.

Communicate clearly and with certainty

For our horses to understand us, we have to develop clear communication with them. We have to make sure that our messages are received.

Be understood to be effective but be effective to be understood. If a horse is not doing what we want, either he didn't understand us well because we weren't clear enough or he simply chose to ignore us and follow his own plan. More often than not it's the first case and only in the last case should we become more firm in our communication; we must be effective.

Be attentive

We need to learn to read our horse's body language. Only then we can accurately assess the information our horse gives us and understand what our horse is trying to communicate.

Because we see our horse as our partner, we want him to feel allowed to express opinions and ideas. I want my horses to know that they can show me when they feel worried, or if they have an idea of their own. This doesn't mean that we have to follow their ideas all the time, just like horses sometimes decide not to follow the idea of another in the herd.

Stand your ground

A leader means what he or she says. You can rely on them walking their talk; otherwise you very quickly lose respect. Sometimes our horses simply have a different point of view or are in a frame of mind where they can put themselves and others in danger.

While we spend undemanding time with our horse in the field, there is little reason to control and correct the horse. All we need to make sure is that he doesn't run over us. But as soon as we take our horse out of his world into our world, we must make sure he listens to what we say for the sake of safety. And we must practice this obedience every single time in the little things so that the day we have to really stand our ground, our horse quits the discussion right away.

Take, for example, crossing a really busy road with your horse. He is afraid of all the cars in front of him and, to complicate things, there is a mom with a stroller approaching from behind. Now he is really scared, and you can feel that all he wants to do is bolt. But this would be dangerous. In a situation like this, we have to stand our ground and be firm and decisive for the safety of everybody—the mom and the child, the passengers in the cars, ourselves, and our horse. If your horse didn't learn to listen and obey your decisions with confidence, this situation will most probably end badly.

Or imagine that your horse is badly hurt and needs the vet ASAP. In this situation, there is no room for other ideas and discussions. He needs to get into the trailer now, especially if his life depends on it, which he can't possibly know. As his responsible leader, we have to make the decision for him and can't leave room for discussion in this situation. Of course, this also means that we need to prepare our horse ahead of time for situations like this.

This is why it is so important that we insist that our horse keeps certain rules of good conduct without questioning them. We have to practice this on a daily basis. Yes, the horse can make suggestions. But if I choose not to follow but to insist on my plan, I don't want my horse to challenge this; I want my horse to learn to accept a no. This, however, doesn't mean that we turn our horse into a robot or that we turn into a dictator. Be as friendly as possible, but as firm as necessary. I will talk a bit more in depth about this aspect in Chapter 11.

Have a vision

One trademark of all great leaders is that they have a vision of where they want to go. This is probably the reason why they turned into leaders in the first place. That's also why the first chapter of this book is about having a dream. If we have a dream, we can let it be our engine and our drive. It will give us determination and enthusiasm. It will help us to have a plan towards achievement.

We, as leaders, should always know where we want to go, what we want to achieve next. If we don't, the horse will simply make his own plans. In a herd, it is either follow or have your own ideas. And if there is nothing to follow, the only thing left is to have your own ideas.

This is why it is so important to keep our dream alive no matter what other people say. We have to break it down into achievable bits and pieces to make it become a realistic goal to reach. This will give us overview, and we will be able to always think one step ahead of our horse. Then he has someone he can follow.

Cultivate self-discipline

One reason great leaders are respected is because they show a lot of self-discipline. We need to follow our goal with determination, but without discipline, we won't get far. Wonderful achievements don't fall out of the sky—they are a product of a lot of disciplined, passionate, and structured work.

We need to have the discipline to follow the plan we have made and not quit when things get a bit difficult. We need to have the discipline to practice the "boring" but important little things as well as work on the more complex tasks.

Overcome frustration

There will be difficulties as with everything in life. The question is: Do we let them pull us down or do we attack them with positive energy? The attitude we have towards difficulties can change everything. Do you choose to complain, beat yourself up and dwell in frustration or do you choose to see difficulties as learning experiences? Every single challenge we encounter is a chance for growth and for learning.

> **"In the middle of difficulty lies opportunity."**
>
> – ALBERT EINSTEIN

With my mare Mazirah, I did a lot of things wrong in the beginning. Things didn't develop at all how I had them imagined. I fell off, I got angry on her; I treated her unfairly and reacted to her rejection of me with negative emotions. I knew in these moments that I shouldn't do that, but I didn't know how to do things differently and how to handle myself. I was overwhelmed by frustration. Frustration starts where knowledge ends.

The answer is to turn your frustrations into your fascination. Finally, I learned to use this frustration energy to get my problem-solving brain going.

There will be times of frustration when we don't know why our horse reacts like this or that, or does certain things. The key is knowledge. Keep learning and educating yourself. The more you know, the better you can be for your horse. Or get help from a professional; a set of experienced eyes can help untangle a very tight knot.

Horses forgive so quickly. They are not like people. They never forget, but they forgive, and they are happy to change when we are. Apologize to your horse and start afresh.

Have enthusiasm and gratitude

A leader radiates enthusiasm and positive energy. But I rarely see owners showing their horse when they are happy about what he did. How come? Maybe we have learned to be too critical with ourselves? Allow yourself to be motivated and enthusiastic about your goal and your dream. Horses will imitate emotion, so you as the leader should be the first to show enthusiasm. Don't wait for your horse to be motivated; pull him into your motivation.

Let your horse know and feel when you're happy and enthusiastic about what he did. Stop criticizing yourself and your horse for every tiny imperfection. Be enthusiastic about the little nice moments and they will magically proliferate. A leader who radiates enthusiasm for his project is easy to follow.

Appreciation, too, will motivate a horse to give more effort. You know from your own life that feeling you've been treated unfairly quickly makes us sour. The same goes for horses. They love it when we show them our appreciation. How often do you reward your horse? How many of the little things that your horse does well do you take for granted? Try one day to reward your horse for every "normal" good behavior, like simply standing still for grooming. Or giving his feet to have them picked. Or just for trotting along nicely. Get in a habit of saying thank you to your horse. It is such a gift that our horses carry us on their backs, so the least we can do is say thank you and reward them for doing what we ask them to do.

Don't take things personally

Horses are horses, not humans. Horses act in the moment. They don't plan, and they can't think in complex ways. Horses don't want to annoy you or pay you back for yesterday's tough lesson. They also won't feel offended if you express yourself and your expectations loud and clearly; in fact, they will appreciate it. Treat your horse like a horse. Anthropomorphism has no place in horse training.

How to become this type of leader

You might feel a little bit overwhelmed by now. And you are right, it is confusing to know how to lead sometimes and be what our horse needs. We tend to have so many doubts about ourselves and see so many areas where we aren't good enough.

Embrace leadership without guilt

In all the years I have been coaching human/horse couples, the most difficult point is being able to set boundaries and insist on them. Somehow there seems to be an enormous block when it comes to this for many, women especially, including me.

Even if we know what we have to do for our horse, and we are able to execute the technique, it somehow still feels wrong. The heart tightens and twists a little when we are asked to be firm. We feel guilty towards our horse. Or there might be occasions when we act badly to our horse because he has annoyed us one time too often. Either way, there might be the fear that the horse is upset with us afterwards and might not like us so much anymore. Guess what? This doesn't help anyone—not your horse and even less yourself. Everybody feels bad.

The thing to do in a moment of irritation with your horse is to come back to awareness. Then ask yourself why you got annoyed in the first place. Mostly we get annoyed when we didn't say no in time or didn't insist on a limit the first time the horse crossed the line. We can be too tolerant. We wait too long before we decide enough is enough. We often try to keep the waters calm, not just with our horse, but in our family and at work, and we tolerate it for so long that people step on our toes or we put up with a poor compromise. Our horse is just a reflection of this.

Why? Why do we value everything else more than ourselves? Why do we give everything else more importance than we give to our own feelings and priorities? Why are we so much more concerned about everybody else's happiness than about our own contentment? Why do we respect everybody else so much more than ourselves?

Have courage to express yourself

This is where I see the real problem. In today's society, girls are raised to not express when they feel uncomfortable. *"Come on, say hello to this man; be polite!" "Come on, that's not so bad, you can do that!" "If you say no, Grandma will feel bad." "Eat up your dinner, your mum put so much effort to make this delicious meal."*

Whenever a woman dares to speak up or to lead, she is frowned upon. Yet, if she were a man, boldness would be praised. It's time for women to be bold, even with our horses. We learnt to ignore our limits and true feelings to avoid others feeling bad. We learnt to tiptoe around other people's feelings, but we didn't learn to take care of our own feelings.

Others always seem to be more important. We forgot how to listen to ourselves. Our inner voice helps us to recognize our limits so that we can protect them and ultimately us. It keeps us safe.

I believe that we only get annoyed with our horse for two reasons:

- We don't know how we should react
- We think we aren't allowed to defend our limits

Let me tell you: Your little voice is right. Listen to it and act on it. You have all the right in the world to let your horse know what you would like him to do or not do! As soon as you feel just a little bit uncomfortable, let your horse know. He can't know otherwise; he can't read your thoughts. And him being a horse, he will just do what comes to his mind in the very moment and do what is possible for him. If we spoke up at the very first moment our horse does something we don't like, we wouldn't need to correct as strongly. Do less sooner, rather than more later. We need to become less tolerant and learn to calmly tell our truth now—out of love for our horse and ourselves, driven by the intention to prevent drama later.

Horses don't overstep our limits on purpose. They don't wake up in the morning and think: "Today I will check if she gets angry when I stand on her foot" or "Let's see how annoyed she gets when I stop to eat grass all the time." It is up to us to let them know what's acceptable to us.

Horses don't mind being told off; it happens in a herd all the time: "Go away, this is my hay, my spot." No horse is emotional or upset about it. They know how to protect their limits in a way that the others don't feel offended or threatened.

Horses will only do what they are programmed to do by nature, what you tell them to do and what you allow them to do. Horses do only what works for them, especially young horses: "This behavior works for me, this doesn't, so I will not do that anymore." This has nothing to do with testing your leadership, checking who is more dominant than the other. Rather, this is merely checking what works and what doesn't. If the first time the horse tries to pull you to a nice piece of grass and it doesn't work, chances are higher that he won't see it as an option anymore. If however you "allow" him to pull you around at the first try, he will see it as an option from now on. Each time he will go for it with more certainty. And if you finally decide to stop him after ten incidents, it will be pretty hard to convince your horse that he isn't allowed to do that anymore. In his mind, he's like: "I have always been allowed to do that, so why suddenly not now? Are you really sure? What if I fight for it?" And this is then the point where we really have a more serious argument with the horse that is upsetting for both. We need to adopt the clarity of an electric fence. Horses usually only touch the fence once, and the fence doesn't get frustrated or angry if a horse touches it—and doesn't run after the horse to shock it again.

Be loyal to yourself first

How many times do you just allow your horse to do things you don't like? How many times do you tell yourself, "Oh, that's not so bad, he will stop soon," and then get super annoyed about it because it becomes a new habit?

To be loyal to ourselves and to learn to listen to and respect our little inner voice: I believe these are the most powerful things we can learn from horses. And by embracing ourselves again, we become authentic and leadership becomes easier.

Say yes to who you are right now. Beating yourself up over inadequacies or things you did in the past will only hold you back. All these "What ifs" and "Shoulds" are just ruining your day. Close the book of guilt and blame. Start a new book, one of freedom, acceptance, and new possibilities.

Allow yourself to *be*. Learn to *be you* with confidence. In this way, you can be like your horse, who is just a horse in a very authentic way. You are okay and allowed to be just as much as your horse is okay and allowed to be. When you understand this, you will also be able to truly listen and give room to your horse.

How horses help us grow

I learned about allowing myself to be with Mazirah. By now you know her a bit—the hot, emotional and sensitive Shagya-Arabian mare I bought as a three-year old. Until I met her, I never had a horse as extroverted as her. I honestly did the best I could. I would listen to her, be kind and soft as much as my own patience allowed. I was holding myself back, not wanting to upset her more until everything was just too much. We were caught in a destructive cycle: I was too tolerant too long and didn't offer her enough guidance so that she could feel safe. At some point, my patience would snap, and I would overreact. Of course, then she got afraid of me and her behavior became even worse. She kept pushing on me, bolting, running around like a chicken with its head cut off. At one point I was completely desperate, frustrated and utterly at my wits end. I felt terribly guilty, knowing that I was the cause of the disaster.

That's when, luckily, I met my mentor Berni Zambail who made me aware that I was caught in a personality mismatch with Mazirah. Her, the crazy extrovert who is never afraid to express herself and me, the quiet and gentle girl who was too shy to really express herself and to speak up. The first time I dared to be more extrovert and engage in a conversation with Mazirah that would make sense to her, it felt horribly uncomfortable. But I could see the results almost instantly. Mazirah was suddenly listening. She started to open up and trust more. As I found and accepted my extroverted side, I was able to be the leader she needed to feel safe.

I knew all along that I had this expressive, energetic, and even playful side sleeping inside me. Mazirah helped me to unlock it, and she helped me to say yes to this side. She showed me that I didn't need to feel embarrassed or shameful expressing myself and my wishes and limits. She showed me very clearly that she wanted to meet the true me, that she wanted to know my opinions, and that she preferred when I expressed myself loud and clear, rather than quietly hoping for her to change one day. I learned to be a bit more the boss mare.

But maybe you are on the other spectrum. Maybe you are an extroverted person who happens to have an introverted and timid horse. This is what happened to my husband a few years ago. He has a very extroverted and self-confident personality. After his horse died, a new horse entered his life. In the beginning, he couldn't catch the horse in the field, no matter what. And the longer it took, the angrier he got, which the horse would sense, of course, which scared him off even more. After a while, my husband learned to listen and to be quiet, to allow instead of control. And then the horse would be confident to come when called. My husband had to develop the lead-horse side of himself. As soon as the horse felt that he was seen and listened to, he was just perfect.

Exercise:
Find your inner leader

Go to chapter 3 of the workbook and explore the reflective questions on "Find your inner leader". If you haven't already, you can download the workbook here:
https://www.understandingisthekey.com/workbook

Or, take out your journal and reflect on whether you are an introvert or extrovert. If you are an introvert, think of ways you can develop the extroverted side in yourself. How can you practice speaking up and acting with certainty and courage? If you are an extrovert, how can you practice allowing and listening?

Whichever side you have to develop, it will feel uncomfortable at first. But if you allow yourself to go into that journey with an open heart, you will find your true self. You will find new confidence you never thought possible.

Your horse invites you to unfold yourself, to discover new possibilities, to dare to be yourself and to value yourself. Our horses help us along the way to become a good leader. Allow yourself to be immersed in the experience. Development takes time. This is your journey. You can choose to enjoy it.

The Power Mindset

W hat is the deciding factor that turns your horse into a dream horse and not a nightmare? To find the perfect stable, the perfect food, to stick with a method everybody tells you that it is good, to work on yourself, to get better and to improve? The responsibility seems huge and the possibilities of failure are many. We spend too much time "What if-ing" and "yeah-butting" and waste so much energy on limiting thoughts.

Instead, we should focus our energy on our possibilities and go forward from there. What do you believe you can accomplish? How often do you catch yourself not doing something because of fear of failure? If you consistently take one little step after the other, you will still reach your goal, but first you must believe it can happen. Don't let fear hold you back. You have to believe in yourself; nobody else will do it for you. You can do way more than you think you can because you already have the right qualities within you.

All successful horse people have one thing in common: their mindset. Adopting what I call the Power Mindset will help you deal with restrictions, feelings of inadequacy, and frustration.

Affirmations for the Power Mindset

1. I have a dream
2. I am a creator
3. I am aware of myself, my horse, and the process
4. I am a natural leader
5. I understand my horse
6. I take it step by step
7. I am empathic

8. I am patient
9. I am a teacher
10. I respect my horse and his/her needs

1. I have a dream

THE MINDSET: *I have a dream and I don't let go. My dream is what motivates me, what keeps me going even if I encounter difficulties. I protect my dream against people who think there are too many reasons why it won't come true. I don't allow anyone to talk negatively about it. My dream makes me jump out of bed in the morning, gives me the drive and passion to make the seemingly impossible become possible. It leads me on my search for knowledge, education, action, and success.*

We have already explored this topic in previous chapters, so here I will simply remind you that not having a dream means you will live a life in mediocrity, without passion, without drive. Be brave and have a crazy big dream. If it doesn't scare you just a little bit, it is not bold enough! Use the power of your dream as motivation to take the right steps.

Everything starts with a dream—every invention, every empire, every great adventure or endeavor. That person with a dream got so passionate about it that it led the person to take the necessary action to make it come true.

2. I am a creator

THE MINDSET: *I know that I was born with the ability to create. I believe in myself and in this God-given natural ability. It is in my hands to create the horse of my dreams.*

It is easy to reach goals when you have big talent and a lot of money. It is easy to go and do stuff when you are self-confident and don't care what others think about you. But when you don't have any of this, or miss one or two, it is hard. I know all these doubts; they can be paralyzing. They cause you to stay on the couch instead to go and enjoy your horse.

The reason we don't manage to do so many things is simply that we give up already before we ever tried. We have so little belief in our abilities. I know it is hard to self-motivate, to self-encourage, but when you discover you can actually achieve what you thought you couldn't, that is empowering! My experience is that if I get up and put my energy and mind to the task I thought I couldn't manage, I would manage. Because we can. Because we have the innate power to create things and use the power of our minds.

Every day it is a new and conscious decision to push all doubts away and take another step towards the dream.

3. I am aware of myself, my horse, and the process

THE MINDSET: *I am aware of my motivations and the why behind my actions. I know why I have a horse and where I want to go with my horse. I know about my completely normal predator reflexes and how to not act upon them. I am aware of my horse's needs. I don't project my humanness onto my horse or try to humanize. I have clarity about what he should learn when and why.*

Everything starts with awareness. Awareness brings clarity to our minds and plans. Clarity brings peace. If I have no awareness, I will run into the same mistakes and roadblocks again and again.

Be aware of your horse's prey-animal nature and how you can trigger his instincts with your predator reflexes. A little awareness goes a long way to avoid everyday troubles.

Be honest with yourself (although this doesn't mean self-judgment). You have the right to be and have your dreams and reasons. No guilt, no shame.

4. I am a natural leader

THE MINDSET: *I know myself, and I value myself, my needs and my limits. I can take care of myself first. This helps me be an authentic, natural leader to my horse. I know about my horse's need for clear rules. I am there for my horse. I am his provider, his caretaker, his protector, and his educator. I am in charge with kindness and fairness.*

Again, we have explored this topic previously, but it cannot be talked about too much! I know that the ability to be a leader is there, in each one of us. It is our job to find and to empower that leader in us. Everything starts with giving yourself and your inner voice value and not blaming yourself for the points where you could improve. Everything starts with saying yes. Say yes to your needs, to your limits, and to yourself.

5. I understand my horse

THE MINDSET: *I understand my horse's nature, how he thinks and how he plays. I know about his unique character, and I appreciate his qualities. I know what I need to do to adapt and to bring out the best in my horse. I understand how to motivate him when he feels bored and low in energy. I know how to help him to feel safe when he is scared and scattered. I know how to make him feel confident about himself and his abilities.*

Horses think so differently than we humans think. It's no surprise that the potential for difficulty is so great! We have to dive deep into the subject of equine behavior. Discover how to read horse body language and study your horse's movement and gestures; every horse is unique. Learn about how to motivate the lazy horse, how to calm down the crazy horse, how to make the tense horse feel at ease, and how to win the cooperation of the naughty horse.

By learning how to correctly read your horse and accommodate him, you will bring out the best in him. This is your key to getting an enthusiastic, confident, and happy horse on your side.

6. I take it step by step

THE MINDSET: *I take one step after the other, even if it is a seemingly tiny, useless step. I keep going, no matter what. There will be times it will be easy, but there will be times it will be hard. I grow through every challenge and failure. I will not dwell on excuses but find the real reason behind them and go to see my horse anyway. I do this for my horse.*

A dream will stay a dream if we don't take the first step towards it. A goal is a dream with a deadline. Nobody can fulfill your dream but you. It is you who must get up, put one foot in front of the other and do the things necessary. Write down your goal and break it down into steps—you can even break down the steps again. Make sure that you don't take too big a step at once; set yourself up for success! This will help you to stay motivated when things get challenging.

7. I am empathic

THE MINDSET: *I am empathic with myself. I allow myself to be where I am and to progress at my speed. I allow myself to make mistakes. I even embrace my mistakes because I know that I will learn from them. I always do things with the best intention, and this is what counts. I am empathic with my horse. I have an open heart for his way of thinking and reacting. I try to think like my horse so that I can see the world from his perspective. I allow my horse to make mistakes because he will also learn from them. I put my heart in my hands and let my actions be motivated by my passion.*

Nobody is helped if you beat yourself up over your mistakes. It only makes you feel terrible and insecure the next time you do the same thing. This doesn't mean ignoring mistakes, but you could just say: "What I just did was not so smart. I will remember this and find a way to act differently the next time in the same situation." Finding out what doesn't work is also learning.

Be empathic with your horse and how he perceives the world from his perspective. Your horse never means to "mock" you or challenge you personally. There is always justified reason behind his behavior. Try to look at the world from your horse's point of view and you will right away have better understanding and more empathy for him.

8. I am patient

THE MINDSET: *I trust the process and our journey together. I am patient for things to fall in place. I know that success doesn't happen overnight, but that success is a process, which I enjoy. I am patient with my own learning and improvements; I know everything will come if I keep going step by step. I am patient with my horse, and I will take the time it takes to teach him everything he needs to learn.*

Impatience makes us unhappy. It is so hard for us to be in the moment and be happy with what we have; we always wish we had already achieved this or that. Be patient for things to work out. Everything takes time with horses. Be patient with yourself and give yourself time to learn things. The worst thing you can do is to push yourself too hard and lose confidence. As soon as you try to push it, things will fall apart.

Be patient with your horse: allow him to learn at his speed, allow his confidence in you to grow slowly, and most importantly, give your relationship time to grow.

9. I am a teacher

THE MINDSET: *I educate my horse so that he knows how to deal with the human world. I teach him certain skills before they become urgent, such as trailer loading, bathing, farrier preps or vet preps. I am in control of the situation, and I am always one step ahead. I think of the future and teach my horse what is necessary so that he can understand later. I educate myself as necessary to reach my dream. I ask for help and support when needed for my horse's sake.*

> *I won't say: I am so clumsy.*
> *I will say: I will master this with time, all I have to do is practice!*
> *I will not say: My horse doesn't like this.*
> *I will say: How can I explain to my horse that this is not so bad?*

Education is the key to understanding your horse. And educating your horse is the key that he can understand you. Mutual understanding is the key to unlocking the door to your dream. If you don't take the time and put in the effort to educate yourself and your horse, you will not reach your dream. Everything can be learned, but sometimes you might need support from the outside.

10. I respect my horse's natural needs

THE MINDSET: *I know about my horse's need for free movement, social contact, and continuous eating. I make sure to fulfill my horse's natural needs first. I know about the necessity and the basics about general care such as deworming, vaccinations, proper feeding, hoof care, dentistry, biomechanics and saddle fitting. I take care of my horse in a responsible and holistic way.*

A horse whose basic natural needs are not fulfilled will not be ready and open for you. His mind will be preoccupied worrying about other things. Either he has too much energy because he was locked in a box, or he is hungry, or he feels frustrated because he doesn't have social contact. Owning a horse and keeping it happy and healthy is a huge undertaking. Horse owners often depend heavily on the advice of professionals, such as their farrier, vet and saddle fitter. Educate yourself so that you can be less reliant on other people's advice. Take it from me: being knowledgeable enough to be independent of others (or knowing what professional to trust) is priceless. Educate yourself on as many aspects of general horse care as you can so that you can make responsible choices for your horse. This will not only save you money in the long run, but also keep your horse happy and healthy for a lot more years.

Exercise:
What if you had unlimited courage?

Whether you reach your goal depends upon your attitude. If you don't believe in yourself, who should do it for you? You can achieve so much more than you think you can right now. But it must start with a decision to be committed. It's a conscious decision, a mindset of doing the things that are necessary.

What would your competent and confident self do in your situation? Go to chapter 4 in the workbook. Take a moment to reflect on what you would do with unlimited courage. What would your decisions look like? Then, print the 10 Affirmations provided in the workbook to place them in a spot where they'll frequently remind you of your Power Mindset!

If you haven't already, you can download the workbook here: https://www.understandingisthekey.com/workbook

Part 2:

Understand Your Horse

THE PREY-ANIMAL HORSE

HORSE PERSONALITIES

EQUINE LEARNING

THE HORSES' NEEDS

The book *Men Are from Mars, Women Are from Venus* by John Gray brought it to worldwide attention that men and women think differently. We all know this from our own lives, of course. More often than not, this difference can make us lose our patience because we just can't understand why the heck he does things the way he does! We know that our partners of the opposite sex are different, and this difference can keep us from having the relationships we want. But if we put a little effort to understand their differences in feeling and thinking, we can go a long way toward a harmonious relationship.

The same is true for our horses. They are just different, perhaps even the opposite of us humans. By learning to understand how they think, feel, learn and perceive the world around them, you will take the mystery out of it all. You will know why your horse acts the way he does, you will become aware of how your behavior either causes your horse to act up or be just perfect. By truly understanding what makes a horse tick, you unlock the door to the relationship you wish for with your horse.

The Prey Animal

H orses are not brave by nature. Everybody into horses knows that horses are prey animals. But what does that really mean? How does a horse, as a prey animal, think and react to its world?

This is especially important to know with your young horse. Your youngster doesn't have much experience with the human world yet, so the raw prey-animal instincts are still very close to the surface and super-easily triggered. A foal is essentially a wild horse, not tamed yet, and simple things can lead to big drama.

Learn to understand how the prey animal horse thinks and feels. Learn about how differently they perceive the world around them than us and you will be able to bring out the best behavior in your youngster.

Often horse owners ask me, "How does he behave? Is he being nice?" I am usually surprised by this question because the horse behaves perfectly. When later I ask the owner why they asked me that, I usually get answers such as, "At home he isn't easy to catch," "He doesn't stand still for grooming," "He is nervous at the mounting block," or "He is impatient when leading."

Why is it that the same horse behaves perfectly with me but not with his owner? It is a matter of triggering the prey animal's instincts. Does our behavior trigger the prey animal or does it bring out the best in the horse? I don't believe that horses identify us humans from a visual point of view as predators; it's our way of acting, especially in stress situations.

How does a predator behave?

Predators are focused on their goal. We want to control everything. When we approach carefully holding the halter behind the back and quickly catch the horse with the rope around his neck, we are being predatory. In stress situations, our view narrows; we focus only on the one important thing. Our hands close quickly and open slowly. Even if now you think, "Oh no, I am not like that," think about when you are stressed, impatient, afraid or angry—predatory behaviors come out, whether you like it or not. It takes self-awareness to fight them and to actively do the opposite.

It is simply a logical consequence that our way of thinking, acting, and reacting very often triggers our horse's instinctive prey behavior. Understanding how the horse thinks and acts and how his instincts are triggered can help you avoid many tricky situations. In every horse live two beings—the one we really appreciate and love, and the other "crazy" or unreasonable one; Jekyll and Hyde. "This is not my horse; usually he doesn't act like this." "Why is he acting like a lunatic?" "He doesn't listen anymore." "Usually he knows how to do this perfectly; he is stupid to not remember anymore." Do any of these statements sound familiar?

It is the phenomenon we experience when our horse is relaxed and calm, not "triggered" in his prey-animal behavior vs. when his instincts are activated and he acts on them. Yes, in a way, there are two horses in one, and we must deal with each one completely differently. The big question is: Which version of our horse do we encourage to show up more often with our own behavior?

How does a prey animal behave?

What are the most important points to keep in mind about the prey-animal horse? Here are the most basic:

- The horse is a social, herd animal, accustomed to a live in a hierarchical social structure.
- The horse is a flight animal.
- The horse is a movement animal, evolved to live in open spaces.
- The horse is an instinctive animal, reacting often out of pure instinct and not out of calculated thinking.
- The horse's senses are highly developed, and their vision is different than ours.

I don't want to go into lengthy discussion about these basic points but stay practical by examining what they actually mean for our everyday life with horses.

Horses are always on the lookout

Even if you think that they are not looking, they are. This one point assured their survival over many thousands of years. Being more vigilant than the wolf, they spot the predator before the predator spots them. That's why so often we have the impression that our horse is hallucinating purple men in the bushes. They stare into the distance, spook at the sight of a shadow or a tiny noise, the list goes on. Horses will always, in a way, be on the lookout for danger.

Of course, there are some who will be more reactive than others, but in general, horses are programmed to see everything. And I mean *everything*. Even if your horse seems to be half-asleep, there is simply never a time when he's not on alert.

Horses will notice every change in their environment

A horse can detect the slightest of alterations in their surroundings. For example, they will spot if the arena has been watered and there are some wet spots on the wall. The day before, the wall had been dry and uniform all the way around. Your horse behaves as if these darker spots are black holes that will swallow him in one piece. Every single time you go by that spot, your horse does the most beautiful side pass at the trot. The spot wasn't there yesterday, and that is proof enough it must be dangerous! My own mare Mayana sometimes acts like this.

Your horse is simply being a good horse by being vigilant to those changes. Yes, I know, this is very annoying. I have a horse who each winter develops a weird fear of blue barrels. In summer, he loves to play with them, jump over them, roll them around. But in winter, I can hardly ride past them without his eyes almost popping out of his head.

Horses will notice every change in their usual environment. Change means eventual danger, so by having excellent memory and observing skills, horses simply make sure they survive.

Change of weather, change of light, change of environment, change of human, change of food, change of the hour you take your horse out—everything is noteworthy to our horses. Be aware of this simple fact, just so that you are mentally prepared to eventually adapt in case your horse reacts to the change.

His first idea will always be RUN

Horses have no horns like other prey animals, such as cows or goats. Their only means of survival are their speed and ability to spot danger. Horses will always run first, think later. But mostly, all they think is: "Phew, I survived, good that I ran." And they will run again the next time. It is simply the innate program that nature gave them to make sure they survive.

The distance a horse runs after a spook strongly depends on the level of the horse's spirit. Some horses, like Arabians, will run longer; some horses, like drafts, will maybe just run a few meters.

We, being predators, will think first and then decide whether it would be smarter to run or not. This is a natural program; the predator must preserve his energy to have some reserves for the next hunt. But he can't know for sure when he will have a successful hunt the next time, so it is smart to preserve energy for when it is needed the most. Horses eat all the time because their food grows under their feet. Therefore, they don't need to waste a lot of energy to replenish their body, and they will run immediately whenever they think there is any kind of danger.

Unfortunately for us, their reaction time is ten times faster than ours. This explains why so often we have the impression our horse spooked "out of the blue." If we try to stop a horse from running by pulling on two reins when his flight instinct gets triggered, we just trigger another fear in the horse: the fear to be trapped.

Horses are highly claustrophobic

As a prey animal, you better not enter a dark cave because that's where the predator lives. And there is no way to escape. Sounds logical, no?

There are so many situations in daily life, which trigger claustrophobia in a horse:

- Being tied up
- Being ridden with short reins
- The rider's legs
- The halter and lead rope
- Being held short for the vet
- On a trail ride passing "narrow" places like houses, between hedges, forest
- Trailer loading
- Being in a stall
- Tightening both reins when the horse spooks
- Telling your horse to stand still at the mounting block
- Trying to slow a hot horse by pulling on two reins
- Approaching objects/things when held or tied, like clippers or fly spray

Whenever a horse feels restricted in his free movement, he will start to feel claustrophobic and maybe fight for his freedom. This is a fact almost everybody knows and experiences when it comes to trailer loading. Horses hate small places for several reasons, including the fact that they can't look around much and won't be able to run from danger if they need to. Now, they don't know that there is no real need to run from danger in our human world. It is simply their innate survival program. Even another few centuries of domestication won't erase that instinct. The younger the horse, the easier it is to trigger the prey-animal reflexes.

In foals, and generally in young horses, this claustrophobia is triggered very quickly. As soon as a foal is held, it will feel the urgent need to fight for freedom. Logical, because a predator would hold it tightly for the sole reason of having it for dinner. Putting a halter on for the first time can be very frightening if it isn't done slowly, step by step.

Foals will try to protect their head, nose, and the area behind their ears. These are the places a predator would go for an easy kill. Any quick and restrictive move in this area, and a foal will panic and fight. That is the reason so many foals and young horses are difficult to halter and lead. The pressure behind the ears and the feeling to not be able to go wherever they want, makes them panic, resist, and fight.

Another common situation that triggers young horses is meeting strange objects during a walk. The youngster gets a bit tight, arches the neck, and bends away from the object. What is our reaction more often than not? Shorten the lead rope to have more control in case the little one seriously acts up. This multiplies the fear of the young horse even more, because now he isn't only afraid of the object, but his claustrophobia is triggered on top. Whenever we shorten a lead rope or rein and start pulling on it when our horse gets afraid, we worsen the fear. Mostly this is paired with by the person getting tight in apprehension of a major spook and maybe losing control as a consequence. Our horses, of course, notice, and a tense predator/human is never a good thing.

Young horses especially orientate themselves on the emotion of the more experienced, older horse. Whenever you are with your youngster, this elder is you. When you get tense at the same time as your youngster, he will have no more orientation. He will get more scared because this confirms in his mind that something really is wrong. It's a snowball-effect: spooked horse, tightening of lead rope, tense human, more explosive horse. One trigger after another multiplies our horse's reaction. How do we solve this disaster and keep them in control for the sake of safety?

Here's what I do. Whenever I see my horse getting tight and looking suspiciously at something, first I will position myself between the object and my horse. I consciously stay relaxed and breathe. I keep my hands from tightening around the lead rope. Eventually, I even give a little more drift if my horse needs to move away a bit more. I talk to my horse and rub him on his neck to let him know that I see that he is worried. Like this, I keep my calm emotion, just like an older leading mare. By not triggering my horse's claustrophobia and flight instinct with a tight lead rope, he will be able to deal with the fright naturally.

Horses establish leadership via movement

I had a big lightbulb moment when reading Chris Irwin's book, *Horses Don't Lie*[3] and stumbled over this fact about movement and leadership. The way he explained it made so much sense to me and explained so many everyday issues we experience with our horses. Horses establish leadership via movement, as opposed to predators who work out who's boss by trying to immobilize each other. Did you ever watch some puppies play? They roll around trying to pin each other down. Their sign of submission is to show the belly and not move any longer.

Although you might be a vegetarian or a vegan, your core nature is still a predator. You still act like one, especially in stress situations. Like for example when your horse spooks and bolts. We can't help it, but our core reflex will always be to try to stop/immobilize our horse when we want to take control. And this has huge implications for our daily relationship with our horses.

Movement is central to the horse's nature. They move to find food, to establish the herd hierarchy, to exercise, to escape threats. Everything in their lives is about movement. Their way of choosing who is the more dominant, or who can be the leader, is by pushing each other forward. I am sure you have already seen that, especially when introducing horses who don't know each other. They will first sniff hello, then squeal, and maybe strike with their front feet, turn and kick, and the one who moves away first gets chased by the other. Who moves who, who gets the best place at the hay, who drinks first, who goes out of who's way—this is how horses establish leadership. It always involves movement.

Think about it for a moment because this point is a big deal. We are unaware how often we try to control our horse by holding it tight or slowing it down. Leading a horse on a short lead rope, rarely giving it the freedom to look left and right, is a perfect example. All this does is trigger the horse's need to move. As a consequence, he will pull and try to get away even more. The problem is solved by using a longer lead rope, giving the horse some room to move and by walking briskly forward yourself. I know this sounds like the opposite of what one should do because it is against our core nature of the predator who establishes control via immobilization.

"Every single time we think we are out of control, our instinct to immobilize kicks in."

But what about the horse who won't go forward and even kicks out when you insist? Well, this horse is simply checking whether you have the ability to push him forward. He is simply playing nature's game and checking who moves whom. By gaining control over your horse's forward movement, you will establish leadership in a way horses can understand. You will never gain control over your horse by restricting his forward movement; control can only be gained by causing him to move forward and directing this movement.

Horses have a high sensitivity to noises, smells and sudden movements

Being prey animals, horses depend on their senses to detect danger. Often, I am left wondering what the heck my horse

> *"Every single time a horse feels that we are trying to immobilize it, we are perceived as a predator and the horse feels the very urgent need to move even more."*
>
> – GABI NEUROHR

saw, smelled, or heard that made her spook because I sure didn't see or hear anything out of the norm. Horses can hear and smell much better than we can.

While our vision specializes in seeing detail, horses' eyes are specialized in detecting movements. This is essential for their survival in nature. They will recognize any movement out of the ordinary, which is one of the reasons many horses are more tense in windy conditions when everything is being tossed about. "Don't be ridiculous, there is no bear in the bush!" we might say, but humans are able to reason; horses are not. Once the survival instinct kicks in, no reasoning in the world helps, but it's important to remember that there is simply never a time when a horse spooks for no reason.

My girl Mayana often spooks from the little lizards running up and down the low stone wall around our outdoor arena. Or sometimes she can hear a mouse under the leaves in the forest and that makes her jump. Yes, ridiculous in our eyes, but it could just as easily be a poisonous snake that could bite her leg when she steps on it. She is simply preserving her life (and yours by association).

We cannot eradicate the instincts nature gave our horses, so it doesn't help to get angry on our horse in moments like this; actually it will make things worse. An angry predator on the back is one of the worst experiences for a horse. A little bit of understanding, a little give in the reins, and a soft rub in moments like this go a long way to calm the horse.

As an exercise in empathy, just imagine somebody spooks you for fun, jumping out from behind a door when you absolutely don't expect it. How would you feel if you were punished for reacting in shock? It just feels so much better to laugh about the spook, to get reassured that there was no real danger. Same with our horses. With Mayana, I adopted the habit of saying: "Hoppala" with a big smile when she does one of her jumps. I rub her, release the reins and my legs for an instant, and let her know that I recognize the fact that she saw something that worried her, and then she can relax because she knows I am aware as well. If in these moments I push her on, I will ride a very tense horse for the next hour.

Horses process three different images

Horses see the world very differently than we do. It's worth remembering that with eyes on the side of their head, horses can see almost all the way around them, but they have "blind spots," namely right behind, above, just in front of their face and under their head and neck.

Due to the positioning of their eyes, they have three different images to process: front, left, and right. Only where the view of both eyes crosses right in front of their head, can horses see three-dimensional and focus on detail. Left and right, on their sides, horses only see two-dimensionally. This means that it is difficult to perceive depth and see details. This is the reason horses will try to face whatever made them spook, for example something along the arena rail. This is also the reason they will counter bend and look to the outside towards where the spook is coming from. Like this, they will be able to see the potential threat three-dimensionally and in detail and evaluate better if it is a serious threat or not.

If you go with your youngster for a walk, for example, and he sees a tree stump on the side of the path, most likely he will snort, bend away from it, push toward you and try to face it. If you insist in this moment that he keeps walking straight, you might blow him up. Allow him to face it so that he can evaluate the situation better. He will discover all by himself that there is no real danger. But just seen in two-dimensions, the tree stump might be a predator crouched low to the ground, ready to attack. Your horse is not stupid for thinking that; he is acting on nature-given instinct. Young horses especially don't have the life experience yet to know that tree stumps are no hungry wolves. You must allow him to learn from experience.

Due to the positioning of the eyes, it is very important to realize that your horse sees the world completely differently left and right. Unlike us, they can't make the connection necessary to make one picture out of the two, which explains why your horse was spooked by a jacket hanging over the arena rail when he passed it to his right, when he was fine passing it on his left. For them, there are two different worlds: one on the left, one on the right. That's why I always do one lap to the left and one lap to the right at the beginning of each session around the arena to show my horse the surroundings with both eyes.

Horses see colors differently

Do horses see colors? Yes, they do, but differently than us. Human eyes have three types of color receptor cells, whereas horses only have two. Scientist Tania Blackmore from University of Waikato[4] studied this. Her conclusion after thorough testing with four horses was this:

- Horses can see a difference between blue and gray, between yellow and gray, and between green and gray.
- Yellow and green look similar to horses.
- It was difficult for the horses to see the difference between red and gray.

In my everyday experience, it doesn't seem to be so important whether horses can see colors or not. They definitely spot the orange of a carrot hidden in my pocket, though! And it seems that the colors blue and yellow are the most visible to them. Whenever I use poles or blocks that are blue or yellow, they will be investigated more. It also seems that when I work with a horse that has some coordination issues, if I put up blue cavalletti, he will be better at looking where he puts his feet. And in jumping competitions the most refusals are on blue jumps.

The horse is a herd animal and highly social

We all get to hear this idea pretty much as soon as we get into horses. But what implication does this have in daily life?

Horses depend on a herd for safety. Every member pays attention to danger, and they will alert each other in case they need to run. Numbers mean safety. Being alone means more danger because it is simply not possible to eat, drink, and sleep all at the same time as watching out for danger. Chances of missing the predator are high when alone.

This is maybe the strongest instinct in our horses. Horses need company to feel peaceful, safe, and happy. This means that whenever you take your horse out of the herd, leave the barn, or go somewhere with him alone, your horse automatically feels stressed. Being alone means being exposed. If your horse doesn't want to come with you or he keeps calling his friends all the time, don't take it personally. His instinct got triggered; he simply hasn't learned yet that when being with you, he can feel safe. With young horses, this is a major point to focus on, so that he/she can learn to be alone with you confidently. When you are with your horse, you form a mini-herd. Ideally, you will be the safety-providing leader, the anchor-point and focus of reverence, just like the old lead mare.

Some horses are real explorers and love to go out and leave the herd, but others depend highly on company to feel safe. If you happen to have the second type, you must condition him to separate from the herd and be alone with you with awareness and attention. Become friends with your horse to the point that he starts to see you as part of the herd. Every time you take him a little further away from the herd, stay away for a longer time. Ensure that the time you spend is interesting but not scary, with lots of praise and fair leadership. Many shorter successful outings will build your horse's confidence to be just with you, away from his herd.

Being left alone is usually worse than leaving other horses. We had a horse who tried to jump over his stall door whenever another horse left the stables, even when there was still another horse in the stall next to him. He started to scream, spin in circles, and rear up. His fear of being left alone was huge. It took a lot of time and exposure to help him overcome this. All logical reasoning, like, "Don't worry your friend will come back" didn't help, but exposing him often to horses coming and going eventually helped him to stay calm because he understood nothing would happen to him when another horse left.

Horses love routines and habits

Routines help horses feel safe. Routines make life predictable, and if you can predict what is going to happen, you will feel secure.

Wild horses form strong habits. Their days have a solid structure of times to eat, times to rest, times of highest activity, and the time to go for water. Change of routine always means that something strange is going on, and this might be life threatening.

For sure, you know these horses who, each morning at the exact same time, claim their morning feed. This is just one example of how much horses are habitual. Anything out of the ordinary, out of the routine, will be perceived as a potential threat. The horse will react with tension, nervousness and stress. Our horses can even sense when our emotional state is out of the norm!

I always rode my mare Salimah in the morning. She was pretty green at that time, not much experience yet. I had a solid routine: get her out of her field in the morning at 9:00 a.m., brush her, tack her up, work her a bit on the ground, and then ride her in our outdoor arena. One day, I could only take her out late afternoon. Already when I came to pick her up, she walked away. And when riding, she was nervous and spooky and wanted to do nothing but run. The change of routine and the fact the light in the arena was completely different (the sun was coming in from a different angle) caused her to be harder to handle. Knowing about her sensitivity to change of habits helps me prepare for events like this, and I might set up the session differently than normal to help her deal with the change.

Some horses just plain don't care, but some horses react very strongly to changes in their routines. What can help horses to react less sensitively to changes is to set up several different routines: one to go on a walk, one to work in the indoor arena, one to work on the cross country course, one to transport your horse somewhere and work there, one in the morning and one in the afternoon. Every routine takes about four to seven sessions to install. After installation, you can change between the routines without your horse getting stressed out about it.

We have to nurture the thinking ability of our horse with awareness to help him to stay present more so that he can think his own way through the scary moments. Horses have the amazing ability to adapt to almost everything.

Exercise:
How can I help my horse feel safe?

So many things in our human world can be perceived as threats by our horse. Everything has the potential to upset our horse and to lead to drama. Does that mean that we should just leave our horses in the pasture? How do we deal with this?

It is not too difficult to help your horse deal with the human world and to overcome his prey animal instincts. It all starts with being aware of what might be triggers for unwanted behavior. Oftentimes, just by being aware, you already act differently and less like a predator.

Go to chapter 5 in the workbook. The questions provided will help you find out how you can act differently to prevent unwanted behaviors and how you can help your horse to be more relaxed in general. Print the page "The 9 Key Characteristics of How Horses Think" and hang it in your tack room. It'll help you remember how horses think and perceive the world around them.

If you haven't downloaded the workbook yet, you can get it here: https://www.understandingisthekey.com/workbook

Equine Learning

C lassical conditioning, operant conditioning, sensitization, desensitization, positive and negative reinforcement, positive and negative punishment, scan and capture, manipulation or sculpting, mimicry or imitation , food or no food rewards …

Horse owners are bombarded with technical terms when it comes to equine learning. It can be overwhelming. Equine learning is a huge topic, which is complicated by the number of scientific terms and the conflicting studies and opinions of professionals. I could explain all those scientific terms to you, but I believe you would end with cramps in your brain and knowing even less how to teach your horse anything. We get too easily drawn into overthinking those kinds of things that we completely forget about everyday, practical life with our horses.

Since I intend this book to be practical, I am going to let you know in simple terms what worked for me and all the horses I've had in training until now. Accompanying notes will mention key scientific terms. If you want to learn more about the scientific learning theory for horses, I recommend Jenifer A. Zelig's book, *Animal Training 101.*[5]

Here are the 13 basic principles I have found to be most important in everyday horse training, inspired by Andrew McLean's *10 Learning Theory-Based Horse Training Principles.*[6]

1. Respect your horse's nature and needs first

As discussed in the previous chapter, we have to learn to thoroughly understand the prey-animal horse and its need for space and companionship, as well as its flight response, social organization and need to forage. This will give us the necessary empathy towards our horses.

We will be able to understand what triggers their prey behaviors and what makes them feel secure and implement this knowledge in our daily interactions and training with our horse. If a horse has no social contact with other horses, is locked up in a stall or little paddock and only receives three meals a day, he will most likely develop some form of stereotypical behavior and won't be able to fully concentrate on learning and his work.

We have to make sure to treat our horse like a horse, not like a dog and not like a human. It is only natural for us to project human thoughts and ways of thinking into our horses. Horses excel at memorizing and recognizing different aids and cues, particularly those that keep them safe. But horses, unlike us humans, don't have the ability to think logically, to make rational connections, to make plans, to draw conclusions. However, we must be careful not to overestimate equine intelligence and say things like, "He knows what he did wrong," especially when trying to justify punishment. At the same time, we have to recognize the fact that horses do have emotions—they can feel proud, fearful, happy, sad, depressed, playful, and content. Horses live in the moment, and they react only to what is happening right now. This is why the timing of reward and consequence is so important.

2. Build your horse's confidence

Before teaching your horse anything, build your horse's confidence. When your horse is new to a place, not very familiar with people, or inexperienced, this is especially important. Give your horse time to get used to the new routines, the new place, the new sounds and people. Then build your horse's confidence with the tools you are going to use.

Make sure your horse is not afraid of the stick or whip you are going to use during training. Also make sure your horse is confident in the environment where you are going to train. Whenever there is a reason for the horse to be afraid, he can't learn. A tense horse will not be open to listening and learning.

How can you show your horse that he doesn't need to fear the stick/plastic bag/fly spray/clipper? Teaching your horse to react calmly in frightening situations is important for both your and your horse's safety. I don't like the word "desensitize" at all. Rather, I like to talk about boosting my horse's confidence and teaching him how to handle scary situations. I like to keep my horse's sensitivity; I don't want my horse to become dull. I would much rather like my horse to get really good at reading my body language and being able to read when something is okay and then trust my opinion.

Keep the following points in mind when teaching your horse to be braver.

A. Approach and retreat

Approach provides the stimulus you want your horse to become accustomed. Retreat creates curiosity and confidence.

Approach doesn't only mean to come closer in a physical way, but also to

- increase intensity;
- increase frequency;
- come closer to a part of the body the horse is more protective about.

Retreat doesn't only mean to quit doing something, it also means to

- decrease intensity;
- decrease frequency;
- bounce ball lower/spray slower/shake flag slower;
- move away from the horse;
- make less noise;
- move away from the body part the horse is more protective about.

You want to rhythmically change between approach and retreat to build your horse's confidence. Retreat when your horse shows signs of worry and re-approach when your horse shows signs of increasing confidence.

B. Relaxation

Relaxation is critical. Do everything with relaxation in your body. Only quit when your horse shows signs of relaxation. Can you identify those signs? A horse that doesn't move isn't necessarily relaxed; it might be tense and frozen. Signs of relaxation kicking back in are as follows:

- Looking at the stimulus
- Blinking the eyes
- Releasing tension in the neck
- Sighing
- Licking and chewing

Observe your horse's eyes: Where does he look? Is he still blinking? A horse that is not blinking is scared and tensed. Reward your horse when he looks at the stimulus so that you teach your horse to confront scary things. The very last sign is usually that the horse licks and chews. If you get to this point, your horse most probably has decided that whatever you did before is okay.

C. Rhythm

Be rhythmic in all your movements. Horses are rhythmic animals. As we humans are predators by nature, we tend to sneak and attack. Be rhythmic in your sequences and repetitions; this will help the horse anticipate what is coming so that he will be able to relax sooner. Try to not scare your horse by sneaking closer and closer with the scary object while talking in a soothing voice. Use a jaunty, nonchalant rhythm in everything you do instead.

D. Release at the right time

Don't quit when your horse moves or reacts with fear. Only decrease the intensity a bit (retreat) and move away from the horse. Release and quit only when your horse gives you one of the five signs of relaxation mentioned above. Otherwise, you will teach your horse that acting on his flight instinct is the solution. The purpose of these confidence exercises is to teach your horse that relaxation and trust are the solution.

3. Use natural learning to facilitate the process

Horses are born super-learners. A foal knows nothing about how to live in the world the moment he drops to the ground. He doesn't even know where to find milk, but he soon learns everything he needs to know. How does a foal learn so quickly? Can we tap into that and use it for our purposes?

The power of curiosity

Being curious is something very normal to all young animals and also to humans. Without curiosity, there is no learning, no interest, no participation; there is only boredom and fear.

The great horseman Tom Dorrance advises, "Never knock curiosity out of a young horse." He is right. This is one of the most important rules in everyday life with foals and youngsters. Their innate curiosity drives them to explore and investigate things. I understand that it can become annoying when they start to empty the grooming box or kick over the wheelbarrow of freshly collected poop. We tend to tell them off too quickly in moments like this. Instead, we should nurture and direct this curiosity, using it to our advantage so that we're not annoyed by it.

"Confidence comes after Curiosity. Allow your horse to be curious about what he was just afraid of."

– Gabi Neurohr

Curiosity develops after fear and flight and opens the door to confidence. The natural chain reaction for a horse is this: He gets spooked by something, then turns to look, and then he gets curious. He will go and investigate and eventually become confident because he realizes that the object wasn't dangerous after all. The beauty of this response is we don't have to do anything to help the process, except provide the stimulus/object (providing that the horse didn't already have a bad experience with this object or stimulus—this would be a whole different story).

For example, you can bring a big plastic tarp or other weird objects into your youngster's field and let him deal with it. You can take him with you when you go with another horse into the arena to ride. Plant all kinds of stuff all around the arena and allow him to explore on his own terms.

Often foals and youngsters will walk into a horse trailer by themselves out of curiosity if we give them enough time. Usually it is us who create the drama by expecting a dramatic reaction from our horse, trying to calm them down and at the same time pushing them to get it done faster.

Setting an object up in a safe way and then letting their innate curiosity work for us allows the youngster to learn in a very natural and easy manner. The more they see and explore at a young age, the less spooky they will be later on. They will be more open to dealing with unknown things and situations.

So, allow your little one to be curious and explore the world, and show him/her lots of stuff. They will learn that whatever we show them is okay.

Learning by observation

Your youngster can learn loads by simply observing and imitating his mother and, later, other herd members too. What horse owners already know was scientifically proven by Janne Winther Christensen, PhD: When you show scary objects to the dam and allow the foal to watch, the foal will show less stress or fear of them in the future.

The study showed that the foals not only got used to those objects they had seen their mother deal with, but the general confidence and acceptance for scary objects was much higher than in other foals the same age. Of course, this only works if the dam handles the objects without fear.

This means if you take an older horse with you and allow your young horse to observe how this horse loads into the trailer or plays with water, he will learn that these things aren't scary or dangerous. Soon, he will try to imitate what the older buddy does.

Learning by imitation

This is how foals learn from the very beginning: imitating their mothers and then other herd members. This is innate behavior; it is natural to them to simply try to do the same thing someone else is doing. The foal will do what his mother does—meaning the better educated and socialized the mother of the foal is, the easier the foal will be to handle. If the mother's attitude towards the farrier, the shower, the trailer, or the vet is relaxed and cooperative, the foal will imitate this and later have the same attitude.

We could use this principle so much more with our youngsters. Almost everybody has an older gelding or mare that has done it all, seen it all. We can make learning, and especially new situations, a lot easier and more relaxed for our youngsters if we take a kind older horse with us.

For example, the first time traveling can be set up for success if you travel your youngster with an experienced and calm horse. Your youngster will take on the behavior and energy of his experienced travel mate and learn that this is not a big deal. The same is true for the first trail rides, or showing scary things, or even jumping for the first time.

You must choose your mentor horse wisely. It should be a truly cool horse, not just one you can control. Horses will not only imitate physical behaviors but also pick up on the emotional state of the older, more experienced horse and show the same emotions.

Learning by imitation will work to a certain extent between horse and human. In my experience, the relationship must be well advanced. The horse needs to have a certain level of confidence toward people. I use this technique mostly to encourage a horse to confront himself with things he might find scary at first. Like entering an unknown stall, entering a trailer, exploring a scary object, jumping a ditch, or navigating through natural obstacles.

4. Know when and how to apply learning techniques

There are two main categories of learning techniques: desensitization and sensitization. In plain English, this means either:

- You want to decrease the reaction of your horse to something (fly spray, clippers, plastic bags), OR
- You want to increase reaction of your horse to something (leg aids, rein aids, etc.).

The main difference between the two techniques is the timing of when to release, when to reward. The second difference is how you apply "pressure" or the "stimulus."

Let's look at an example to paint a clear, practical picture: The Fly and the Fly Spray.

You would love it if your horse responds lightly to your leg aids—just the touch of a fly. But you hate it when your horse reacts with the same avoidance to the fly spray.

- To sensitize your horse, you want to apply pressure gradually in phases. Start as light as a fly, gradually increase and release immediately when you have a response. The release/reward is at the exact moment your horse moves in the desired direction.

- To desensitize your horse to fly spray, you want to keep up the spraying in a soft but consistent and rhythmic manner until your horse stops moving around. The release/reward is at the moment your horse stops moving and is relaxing.

Very often I see people using these two key techniques in the opposite way and are confused and helpless when their horse keeps reacting with panic to the fly spray and doesn't respond with softness to leg aids.

Get aware of what and how you apply learning techniques.

5. Yes and no cues

You want to be able to clearly communicate to your horse if he/she is on the right track or to warn him/her before correcting more strongly when unwanted behavior occurs.

For a long time, I trained without voice cues. Horses aren't verbal, so it's not natural to them to be talked to. I still agree with that. Our body language, intention and energy are still more important than the voice cues we use, and they are certainly not as easy to train on voice cues than dogs, for example.

Still, try to use voice cues without any emotion in your voice, and your horse probably won't respond. As we humans are so verbal, it is only natural to us to express our emotions in our tone of voice. This means, your tone of voice when using these two cues is more important than the words you choose. It is also more important than always using the same word. It's best to use the same word, but intonation and the emotion we put into it seem to be more important to horses, in my experience.

I don't use many voice cues, but I am a big fan of two cues in particular: My "jackpot word" (yes cue) and my "don't do that" (no cue).

The yes cue

With this voice cue, I can let the horse know the following things:

- Encouragement (he is on the right track to the good solution)
- Approval (he did something perfectly right)
- Enthusiasm (how happy/proud I am of him)

For the yes cue, or my "jackpot word" as I like to call it, I use "Good girl/ boy!" Use whatever comes naturally to you when you want to express that you are sincerely happy about your horse. Maybe it is "Perfect!" or "Yes!" Put all your heart in your voice; let your horse know that you're happy and proud of what he is doing. Express your enthusiasm, as if you won a jackpot.

When teaching your horse this cue, you want to combine it at first with a reward such as: scratches, rest, or cookies. Over the course of a few sessions, you will notice your horse pricking his ears as soon as you say your jackpot word.

When you use this consistently, this alone can have a highly motivating effect on your horse. A reward, such as a carrot or scratches or release, will always be a few seconds late. By using this cue, I can communicate with way better timing leading to better and faster results.

My horses love to know and feel that I am happy and proud of them and their efforts. The psychology term for this would be Positive Reinforcement. The click from a clicker has the exact same effect, just with the disadvantage that I need one hand to hold the clicker.

The no cue

This voice cue will help me to do the following things:

- Stop unwanted behavior.
- Give him the chance to change his mind before I correct the unwanted behavior.

- Give him a warning before I correct him more firmly.
- Reduce anxiety and fear caused by sudden corrections for unwanted behavior.

For the "don't do that" cue, I like to use a sharp "Hey" or "No." Use whatever word comes naturally to you. Put certainty in your voice. Don't overthink it, as you will need this cue mostly when there is no time to think.

Sometimes we must correct and be firm our horses—even with our youngsters. If it comes to a situation like this, do your horse a favor and give a verbal warning, i.e., the no cue about one or two seconds in advance. This gives your horse a chance to change his mind and not act out what he/she was about to do and there's no need to get too firm.

When my mare, Mazirah, had her foal, Maserati, I was fortunate to observe how she handled unruly or bad behavior. Always before she would give him a corrective bite, she would warn him up front with a squeal. And when he listened, she would not bite him.

TIMING IS CRUCIAL HERE: You have to give the warning the instant you see that your horse is about to cross a boundary—not after it already happened. If your horse still oversteps the boundary after the warning, you get firm in a way that your horse understands the message. I match the intensity the horse puts into it: the bigger the action the firmer consequence. Your response should be proportionate and not emotional.

6. Teach your horse to yield from pressure

By nature, horses are programmed to push against pressure, not to yield to it. Of course, this so-called opposition reflex is not very practical in daily life. This reflex is the reason so many horses fight the bit, go against the leg, refuse to go forward, don't stop, etc. When horses respond this way, it has nothing to do with them being naughty or not respectful enough. It's simply an innate program, which surfaces especially when the horse is fearful, stressed or otherwise triggered in his prey-animal instinct.

You have to "reprogram" your horse. You must teach your horse to adopt a different reflex—a positive reflex of yielding from pressure. I like to talk of two kinds of pressure:

- Steady pressure when you are touching the horse. All leg aids, rein aids are steady pressure.
- Rhythmic pressure when you aren't touching the horse. The use of a whip/stick when lunging or riding is rhythmic pressure, or when playing at liberty.

Yielding to pressure often has a slightly bitter taste for many horse people. In many people's minds, it involves force, dominance, teaching the horse respect, being strong on the horse. Yielding to pressure has nothing to do with force or fear. It is all about teaching the horse a new program.

It's never about the exercise in question. It's always about the horse's ability to be in conversation and his understanding about yielding to pressure. Whenever you teach your horse to yield from pressure, you need to apply the pressure gradually. Start with a touch that is as light as the touch you wish your horse will respond to one day (your dream aid) and increase slowly but surely and firmly until your horse responds. If you apply the pressure too harshly or too quickly, you cause opposition reflex and your horse won't be able to respond in a thinking way.

"You want to be able to mobilize every part of your horse's body separately, back him up and send him forward with ease. This will be your ABC, your alphabet, you can use to form words and then phrases as you progress in your training. Every sophisticated maneuver is a combination of those basic yields."

– BERNI ZAMBAIL

It's the release that teaches

The right timing for the release is crucial for correct and quick results. Release as soon as your horse responds the right way and repeat until you get a light response from your horse. Timing is everything because your horse will connect to what he did just before the release, with what you expected him to do as a response to the signal you gave. If you release when your horse was heavy, your horse will not learn to be light. Or, your horse just did two or three good steps, but your release was late and just when he did a not so good step. Your horse won't learn as fast as he can if your release wasn't perfectly timed.

In psychological terms, this technique is called Negative Reinforcement. However, there is nothing negative about it. Negative simply means that you are "taking something off" when you get the desired response e.g., the feel/pressure you applied with your hand, leg, rein or stick.

7. Reward your horse

How do you let your horse know that he did the right thing? Just by releasing the aid/pressure? This is one way to train, and you can get some results for sure. But if you want to add spark and to get your horse's enthusiasm up, you need to motivate your horse by giving him a reward he appreciates.

We all want a horse that works with us, that wants to do things with us, and that gives us the feeling that he enjoys to be with us. This is where rewards come in.

Our brains function very much the same: Our boss tells us what our job is, what he wants us to get done, and in the end, we want some sort of gratification—a "thank you," "well done," and, of course, our paycheck. We can do a certain amount of time without, but we tend to get sour and fed up pretty quickly if we feel that nobody appreciates our work.

Horses also work better and with more enthusiasm if you give them a reward. Now, every horse is motivated by different things. Some horses love treats, some horses love scratches, some horses love to have a little break, some horses love it if they are allowed to play their favorite game with you, some horses simply want to feel safe. You must know your horse and find out what motivates him.

What reward fits your horse?

Extroverted and more confident horses are usually motivated by play. Oftentimes, if you start to give food reward to this type of horse, they turn into snappy crocodiles if you aren't super cautious! But they love to play. This means that after having completed difficult exercises that asked for a lot of concentration, you allow your horse to go for a fresh canter on long reins.

Introverted, less confident horses are usually motivated by helping them to feel safe and comfortable in what they are doing. Talking softly and stroking them on the neck while standing by their side is usually a good reward for them. Some respond well to cookies, and usually these types never get annoying about food rewards—they are too polite.

These are just two examples to illustrate how horses respond differently to rewards. You can read more about the different personalities in the next chapter.

8. Be consistent and clear

Your aids and signals should be easy to keep apart for you horse: A means A and B should always mean B. Otherwise, it can be extremely confusing for your horse. This means that you have to be aware upfront about how you are asking for things from your horse. This is absolutely crucial for your horse's confidence in you as a leader. If you aren't consistent and clear in the way you communicate, your horse will find it hard not only to understand you but also to trust you and to be fully confident with you.

Signals

Get clear about what signal/aid you are going to use and what response you want your horse to give. Make a list if it is very difficult for you. Signals need to be easily to be differentiated by the horse – A needs to be always A and B needs to be always B. Horses need us to be black and white—no grey, no maybe. If you ask your horse to back out of your space, you actually want him to back away. Too often I see owners who move backwards themselves or who quit asking when the horse just lifted his head and neck and seemingly backed out of their space.

Be consistent in what you ask; don't start asking for something and then change your mind about it or, even worse, change the way you are asking for a certain exercise and expect the same outcome.

Body language

Being clear starts in our mind. Often, we are simply not clear because we don't have a plan and just want to move our horse around. Get clear about your objective first, then you will be able to be much clearer in your body language. Try filming yourself to see what you are doing with your body so that you can correct any issues you see.

Energy

Horses respond extremely well to our intention and energy and what we radiate. If you want your horse to speed up, raise your own energy. If you want your horse to slow or to stop, relax your own energy. For example, some riders have the issue that their horse won't stop, and when I ask them to show me, I see them holding their breath, being tight in their upper body, and tightening the reins—not relaxing as they should. Using your breath helps you gain more awareness.

9. Form good habits

Horses thrive on predictable habits and routines. Anything out of the norm worries them. Teach your horse helpful habits. Young horses especially appreciate consistent routines. Knowing what is coming and what to expect helps a horse to be calmer and less excited and, therefore, learn faster.

When I teach my youngsters to be confident enough to leave the herd with me, I always follow the same routine. I take the same way to the stables, I ask them to stand still in the grooming corner, I brush them and pick their feet, and finally lead them into the shower. After a few repetitions even the most excitable youngsters calm down because they start to know what to expect. I am installing solid good habits of everyday life.

Later on, when progressing your horse's education, you can apply these routines also on your riding work. When teaching new exercises, establishing a clear pattern helps to accelerate the learning process. For example, when working on trot-halt transitions, always ask for them at the same points around the arena. Soon your horse will anticipate and be mentally ready at those points for the transition

Repetition

If you want your horse to not only learn something but to also complete the exercise consistently well, you need to repeat it often. In general, it takes about three tries until a horse "gets" a new exercise. But then you need to repeat to anchor the new exercise and to form a solid and reliable good quality response.

It takes about between four and seven sessions on the same subject, depending on the horse, to form a consistent response. After that, you still want to repeat every other session for a while until the specific task became part of your horse's foundational repertoire.

10. From easy to complex

Start with easy and progress to more complex maneuvers. Always think about how you can break your end goal down into mini steps. Practice those mini steps, your ingredients. Then slowly put them all together, and seemingly difficult tasks suddenly seem easy. Let me give you an example.

Trailer loading

- Teach your horse to pass over different surfaces, such as a tarp, a wooden bridge to get him used to stepping on noisy surfaces.
- Teach your horse to pass through narrow passages.
- Teach your horse to back up over a pole.
- Teach your horse to back up through a narrow passage.
- Teach your horse to walk under a tarp.
- Teach your horse to yield forwards when applying pressure where the butt-bar would sit.

Prepared like this, chances are way higher that the horse learns quickly to load and show less avoidance behaviors, which are most of the time caused by fear or lack of understanding.

You always need to know where you are going. This will help you to know what to practice and to build step by step.

Screw perfection!

First tries don't have to be perfect. Perfection comes with understanding and repetition. Spare your horse and yourself the frustration of wanting to be perfect. First tries are good enough if you see that it's going in the right direction. If your circle is still egg-shaped or your sideways isn't 100 percent regular, that doesn't matter. With repetition and practice, circles will get rounder and your horse will get more coordinated when yielding sideways.

It's much more important your horse responds and tries to do the right thing immediately, rather than getting it right first time. Shape the response slowly as you go along. Perfect willingness is more important than perfect execution.

11. Bring your horse into a learning frame of mind

Horses can't learn and be attentive when they are afraid, stressed, anxious, bored, unmotivated, or too energetic. Pushing a horse too hard or trying to train a horse with force, and fear won't lead to the horse learning anything except being afraid of training and people. We have to do everything possible to limit the level of excitement during a training session.

At the beginning of each session, help your horse enter a learning frame of mind. Do whatever it takes so your horse can calm down, be confident with you and the environment, and feel motivated. Or maybe your horse first needs to play and get rid of some excess energy before he can listen and learn.

In every session with every horse, I take the first ten minutes to evaluate my horse's emotional state that day and help him into a learning frame of mind. A horse in this state of mind is confident, curious, attentive, and responsive. He will learn quickly and easily. In the next chapter, I will explain in more detail how to help different types of horses to come quickly into this state.

12. Give your horse time to process

Just like us, horses need time to process information, especially when you teach something new to your horse. Give him a moment to think each time you see an improvement in response.

It is perfectly normal for your horse to be a little unsure when learning new things, just as you are too. Watch out if your horse licks and chews, sighs, or if he is blinking. These are all signs that your horse is relaxing about the task.

Get good at reading your horse and the subtle signs and facial expressions he shows you. The better you get at this, the better your timing will be and the faster your horse will learn.

Remember the following visual cues that indicate tension:

- Not blinking regularly
- Tight lips
- Stiff ears or moving quickly
- Wrinkles around eyes or nostrils
- Still facial expression
- Tense neck muscles
- Eyes averted from you

These are signs of low to medium-level tension and excitement. To see signs like this is pretty common, especially when teaching new things or when dealing with young and inexperienced horses. Oftentimes, if you ignore the cues and keep pushing on, a big blow up will follow.

It is simply not possible to keep our horses always in a super-relaxed state of mind. Because horses are so sensitive to changes and are on the lookout for danger constantly, the simple act of taking them out of their herd can cause tension. Does that mean we should leave them in their field all the time? No. We must show our horses how to deal with the human world and how to deal with stress. Apply this to yourself. New things are stressful, new people are stressful, new places are stressful, but will you get better at dealing with these by sitting on your couch and reading books about them? No. Only exposure and confrontation will help you to get confident in dealing with these stressful situations.

From nothing comes nothing. If you don't expose your horse to a certain level of excitement/novelty/stress, he won't have the opportunity to learn how to deal with this. He won't have the opportunity to grow in his self-confidence.

In order to learn and to expand their level of confidence, we have to take our horses out of their comfort zone—not too much, just a bit further every time. Just enough that they can still handle it and gain more confidence as a consequence. You will learn more about this in the last chapter.

Signs that indicate release of tension and relaxation:

- Blowing out
- A deep sigh
- Blinking
- Looks at you
- Lowers head and neck
- Softens neck muscles
- Licking and chewing
- Yawning

Place your rewards on these signs because then you know that your horse didn't merely complete a physical task but did so while mentally and emotionally relaxing. Relaxation is key—mental, emotional, and physical.

13. Pass responsibility to your horse

Teach your horse that he is "responsible" to keep gait and direction and look where he puts his feet. This will avoid having to keep using your leg and rein (or stick and rope) aids constantly and taking control all the time. If we use an aid continuously, it turns into desensitization and the horse will stop responding; the aid becomes just noise. Or, on sensitive/hot horses, it has the opposite effect: they get overstimulated and crazy.

By teaching your horse to keep going, you can avoid both overreacting and dull responses. Start at the very beginning to teach your horse to keep gait when lunging/circling. Can your horse trot for four laps without you pushing him on? Later on, this leads to your horse maintaining canter circles, lateral movements, and even passage and piaffe. The French masters called this "descente de mains," a test to see how truly the horse was on the aids. For a short moment, all leg and rein aids are discontinued, and the horse is supposed to maintain posture, balance, and movement.

Initiate an exercise/movement and leave it up to your horse to continue until you ask for something else. Renew the request only when your horse stops maintaining gait and direction you asked for. Of course, at first, the renewals of aids will be more often, and your goal should be to get more steps/laps/meters with every repetition. This even applies to simply tasks such as standing still for grooming: Direction: facing forward. Gait: Standing still.

It's a question of self-discipline and awareness to stop yourself from constantly using your leg on a slow horse for example. But it is so worth the effort to teach your horse to take responsibility. Your time with your horse will be more harmonious, less of a workout, and more peaceful for both of you.

Stop nagging and start being partners!

Exercise:
Keep the 13 points in clear view

Horse training is simple, but it's not easy ... that is a sentence I hear quite often from my mentors. Yes, you can absolutely get brain cramps if you think deeply about this subject. Keep it simple, use commonsense, and apply those 13 points to nurture the partner in your horse. Learn these 13 points until you know them by heart. Build confidence, establish a language, find the right reward for your horse, be clear and teach your horse to "keep going," and you will be on a good path to teaching your horse everything he needs to know to become your best partner.

Go to chapter 6 in the workbook, reflect on the questions and print the page "The 13 Principles of Equine Learning" for display in your tack room.

Your Horse's
Unique Personality

Your horse is unique, but I didn't have to tell you that. Every horse has his own special personality, just like you and me. Some are more expressive and loud, some are quiet and timid, some are laid back and easy going, and some are funny and playful.

And that is a problem. Why? Because this means that we can't just apply the same training method to every horse. Wouldn't it be so much easier if one method would fit all horses? This is unfortunately not the case. Every horse is motivated by something different and has different strengths and weak points. Every horse has a different level of sensitivity, intelligence and spirit. And this is why some people love a certain method and the same amount of people can't get it to work for their horse. The first time I learned this concept was from Linda Parelli.[8] It makes so much sense when she explains which learning strategy to use for what type of horse.

French scientist Lea Lansade[9] has also studied the different personalities of horses and how they each prefer different training styles. This means that you can learn to understand what makes your horse tick, what motivates your horse, and his deepest fears. You can learn to adapt to your horse's unique personality and learning style.

By knowing the four main personality types, you can learn how to give your horse exactly what he needs, no matter what the situation. Your horse will learn faster, be more confident in you as his leader, be calm, and be more willing and motivated to work with you.

Best of all, though, your horse will feel respected and seen as the individual he or she is. And you will be able to bring out the best in him/her.

The 4 main personalities

Some horses love to move and to run, and there are some horses who prefer not to have to move their feet. These are the first two categories: extroverted and introverted.

And then there are horses who are tolerant, curious, and "bombproof" who don't know what it means to spook, versus the horses who hear the mouse under the leaves and who seem to see weird purple men in every bush they pass. These are the next two categories: confident and unconfident.

If you mix them up, you get the four personalities:

- Extroverted and confident
- Extroverted and unconfident
- Introverted and confident
- Introverted and unconfident

Before I lay out in detail the personalities to you, I want make three important points:

1. **Don't put your horse in a "box"**
    Your horse's personality is not static. It changes depending on circumstances and situation. Just because your horse is mainly confident extrovert, doesn't mean he can't be completely crazy on one day. You have re-evaluate every minute, every day, and in every situation. These are just guidelines; every horse is his own unique mix.

2. **This is not an excuse**
    It's too easy to say: *My horse is crazy in new environments; this is why we can't compete. My horse is introverted, that's why I can't expect him to canter for more than a few strides.* Yes, every horse has his weaknesses, but this is not an excuse. Use the tips and strategies to help your horse overcome his weaknesses.

3. **Evaluate your horse in five categories:**

- At home (known environment)
- In the herd
- With humans
- As a learner
- In unknown environments and stressful situations

Your horse can show completely different characteristics depending on situation. You have to adapt accordingly.

I will introduce you to each one of them, provide example to illustrate that type of horse, and then explain what they find difficult and what their innate strong points are. You will discover what the main problem is you will need to work on and what strategies work for that kind of horse.

Let's start with the extroverted types of horses.

What is true for both the extrovert confident and the unconfident type is that they both love to move their feet. They are forward and they have good work ethics. This is usually the horse that gets ridden with big bits because he is hard to stop. They seem to never get tired and often get described as "hot." The difference between the two of them is that one runs because he thinks it's fun, and the other one because he got scared. One is playful exuberant, the other one is a crazy runner.

The extroverted/confident horse

This type of horse is best described as athletic, funny, creative and charismatic. He will put his nose into everything, including pockets and people. That's why many people would describe this horse as dominant and pushy. But it is much fairer to say that he simply knows exactly what he wants and is super-curious about everything that's going on around him. This leads to the problem that often he wants to do just the opposite of what you want him to do. He is active and loves to be busy, both with his mind and body.

A few years ago, I had the pleasure to start a gelding, Touareg, with just this mentality. He was so full of himself and his ideas that it was hilarious … to a point. Whenever I "dared" to ask him to do something I wanted, he would take me sand skiing by galloping away sideways in a perfect demonstration of his athleticism. I had to find the right strategies to get him to a point that he *wanted* to try *my* ideas, not just his own. Whenever I argued with him and got too strict, I was lost—he would buck and fart, canter sideways, and pull all kind of tricks. I always knew that he was a genius, but the big question was: "How do I get him to put just as much effort into my ideas as his own and be a bit more obedient?"

Difficulties

These horses have a hard time being obedient and willing to do exactly what you ask them to do. They are very confident, and most of the time they have and clear opinion about everything. Especially about what they want or don't want to do. And when their opinion isn't aligned with what you want them to do, it is very easy to get into a real argument.

It is easy to get very annoyed with a horse like this. They are constantly busy doing something— not one moment of peace, always a counterproposition. And when calling them to order, the best we get is a crappy expression or some form of protest. They don't like to work with discipline; repeating tasks more often than three times is almost a punishment for them, and they will just find ways to make the exercise more fun for themselves. Consistency makes them sour, and they get bored very quickly. They can be extremely athletic, especially when expressing their dislike for what you want them to do.

Strong points

These horses are amazing partners if you like variety, action and speed. They are bold and brave and aren't much bothered by being somewhere else. They are eager to discover new things and generally love to work. Jumping, eventing, reining, working equitation (ranching skills), barrel racing, speed trail and high-level dressage are disciplines which suit them well. They love anything with variety, action and a chance to show off.

Paired with their charisma and generally friendly nature, they are often stable favorites. They tend to be very intelligent, fast learners and playful. Emptying the grooming box (don't know if that's a strong point!), "helping" when mucking out and being a joker in general are fun for them, and they brighten almost everybody's mood. This horse will certainly make you laugh and shed tears of desperation at the same time.

Goal

Their main weak point is not being willingly obedient to doing your ideas. The main goal for their mental and emotional development would be to reach a point where they enthusiastically do what you ask them to do.

Key strategies

To bring out the best in this horse, you must think creatively:

1. **Teach new things.** Teach him something new at least once a week. Be progressive. Nothing is worse for this horse than boring routine. If you don't teach him something new, he will find out how to do existing exercises in a new, more creative way—and usually we don't love that so much. So, plan ahead so you can always be one step ahead of this horse.

2. **Variety is the spice of life.** Routine sucks, but soft and perfect and slow sucks even more for this horse. Keep your sessions active, interesting, and playful. Keep your sessions moving forward, increase the pace when your horse is feeling very playful. Lots of transitions, changes, and obstacles will help you to use his energy in a positive way instead of shutting him down for being too energetic.

3. **Screw "perfect."** This horse doesn't see the point in repeating a task until it's perfect. He will pick up on the general idea almost immediately. That's good enough. You will be able to improve the task in every session when you repeat it once or twice. This is not the horse for perfectionists—this is a horse for expressionists.

4. **Teach him tricks.** This horse loves to play tricks. Oftentimes they are very mouthy and very busy in their minds. Teach him some tricks on purpose, like picking up brushes after he emptied the grooming kit.

5. **Praise him a lot.** Every horse of that type got addicted to my laughter. He will love to feel that you are having fun as well! Praise a lot, rubs, smiles, scratches, voice, whatever. Just express whenever you are happy and proud of him in an extroverted way! But pay attention that you reward especially when he is doing what *you* want.

6. **Don't argue.** It's too easy to have an argument with this horse. Just don't. If he goes bucking, ride the waves and laugh, rather than

trying to discipline him, and then ride forward. Telling this horse off is one of the main reasons he misbehaves. Learn to channel the energy. When I play at liberty with my mare Mayana, she first has to run around, bucking, rearing, changing directions, and just generally being very undisciplined. If I discipline her in this moment, she gets very grumpy and doesn't connect. But when I start with, "Yes, good girl" and even encourage her a bit, she will very quickly come to me with a proud look on her face and ask me about my ideas. Encourage their ideas first, and they will get interested in yours. Mold and shape, be happy with "kind of" at first, and get more from him as the session advances.

7. **Give them purpose.** Give them a real job, something to do so that he can understand the why. These horses love cross country, or a trail course, or to work a cow, or jumping against the clock. As soon as there is a clear objective (and a proud human afterwards) their attitude changes.

8. **Go forward.** Move their feet, and you will win their mind. Trying to control him when he is full of play and energy has the absolute opposite effect of what you want to achieve: he gets worse. Be brave, send him forward and have fun! Sometimes they just act foolish because we try to slow them down and control them. Mayana likes to act that way each time I ride her on the cross. When warming up at the walk, she will "spook" over every blue flower and dark-green leaf. The moment I let her go forward, trot and canter, she is perfectly happy.

The extroverted/unconfident horse

This horse is very sensitive and reactive. Innate instincts are close to the surface and easy to trigger. He is easily spooked, and most of them have the same "spooky corner" in the arena for years. His brain goes at a 100 miles an hour, and focusing on one thing is difficult for them. They are fast and athletic, very responsive to aids. Usually horses of this type are tough and never seem to get tired. They have incredible work ethics. If you manage to make them feel safe with you, they will give you 150 percent of their heart and effort.

My mare Mazirah is a perfect example for this type of horse. She was always very forward and would notice any shape, noise, or shade out of the norm. Usually she would respond by running faster and faster. The more I tried to hold her back, the more tense she got, which in return caused her to run even faster. That's how we ended in many dangerous situations: big spooks and bolts even through a village or over busy roads. Once she even fell because of a spook in the corner of the arena.

Once I discovered how to not trigger her instincts and how I could help her to trust me and to relax, she turned into a very enduring, high-performing mare who would put all her heart into whatever I asked her to do, including stopping a whole herd of cows!

Difficulties

Horses like this are flighty, spooky and have quick reflexes. They see everything, hear everything and respond to everything. They are easily confused when they don't understand and respond with tension, flight and general "craziness." Once this instinctive side is triggered, thinking is very difficult; the horse acts on pure instinct.

You can often see horses of this type wearing big bits because they are hard to control. They also easily develop stereotypical behaviors, such as cribbing and weaving due to stress and not enough turnout.

Strong points

Horses of this type bond very strongly to the human they trust. As they look for a leader who can give them safety, they happily accept you once you take that position. Then they will give you their heart and soul. You can ride these horses with the power of your thoughts when they are connected, focused and calm. They are very light and responsive to the slightest suggestion. Many endurance horses or race horses are from this type. They love to run, and they will also go over their limits if you let them. Enduring and tough horses, sensitivity and bonding are their main characteristics.

Goal

The main goal for this personality would be to teach the horse to relax, focus, and trust both in you and the task you ask him to do. It is important to convince your horse that you are his friend, that he can trust you no matter what, and that all your intentions are friendly. Then he will be able to relax and to focus on what you want him to do.

Key strategies

If you want to bring out the best in this horse, you need a lot of quiet patience and loving reassurance.

1. **Consistency is key for this horse.** Routines, repetitions and predictability will help this horse to know what is coming and relax. Variety and action are very upsetting for this horse because he can never know what will come next. You want to keep routines and the general structure of your sessions the same.

2. **Build confidence.** Get your horse used to and confident with as many different objects, noises, tools and so on that you possibly can. The more your horse can be confident with scary things, the more he will trust you no matter what you present to him. You want to have a very solid communication with your horse about when things are okay and nothing to worry about.

3. **Focus on relaxation**. It's too easy to go into your horse's crazy energy and to feel stirred up too. Keep breathing, keep your voice down, keep moving slowly—even (and especially) when your horse has a crazy attack.

4. **Be friendly, always.** Even if you have to act fast and firm at times, keep a friendly spirit and don't take anything personally. Just don't get angry at him for acting "crazy;" he is only afraid.

5. **Interrupt the pattern.** Stop crazy behavior as soon as you see it emerging. You can do this by changing directions, sideways movements, partial and complete disengagements. This interrupts the pattern of flight and your horse is almost "forced" to think, even if just for a second. That way you can re-establish control without interfering with your horse's face, such as pulling on two reins or holding the lead rope short and tight, which they fear the most.

6. **Gradual exposure.** If you always keep this horse in his little comfort zone, he won't ever get braver. But don't overexpose him either: find the fine line in between.

7. **Approach and retreat.** If this horse stops, it's his way of telling you that he is afraid of something. Don't push your horse over his threshold. Reactions like rearing, even flipping over, are very likely to come next. Use approach and retreat instead to help your horse to get confident.

8. **Use circles rather than straight lines.** Ride lots of circles, turns, and serpentines to calm and relax this horse. On straight lines, this horse usually just speeds up, so avoid straight lines until your horse has learned to control himself.

9. **One rein for control.** Don't try to slow him down by pulling on two reins. This will trigger his claustrophobia, and he will want to run even more. Nothing is worse for this horse than to feel held and restricted. I know this from personal experience. Trust me, putting a harsher bit and pulling stronger doesn't help in the long run. Use one rein for control, ride circles, and bend your horse to slow his momentum.

10. **Be certain and clear.** Don't be passive and hesitant with this horse. He needs your leadership, so he needs to know that you have a plan and know what to do. Be firm but friendly. Act certain.

11. **Keep excitement levels low.** Don't try to teach anything while he is still excited and tense; he won't be able to think. Before teaching anything to this horse, you first need to have him calm and connected to you.

Now let's talk about the introverted types of horses. When it comes to both introverted/confident horses and introverted/unconfident horses, both types are rather low in energy. They don't have much get-up-and-go; they are more laid back. This is not the horse that will be hard to stop or that will run off at speed. If they get a chance to take a rest or to slow down, they will take it. The difference between the two is: One of them doesn't see why he should move, and the other one is too scared to move.

The introverted/confident horse

The introverted/confident horse is the classical lazy guy. The more you kick him to go, the more he slows down. This horse is asking, "Why should I do that? Is your idea really better than eating hay?" If you find yourself working a lot more than the horse, your horse is probably this type. This horse appears to be stubborn, lazy and greedy. But he is also reliable and sturdy. He is tolerant and kind; he just prefers to not move too much too fast.

My first encounter with a horse like this was with one of my first ponies—a Fjord gelding named Lotus. At first I thought he didn't want to go forward because of his lack of fitness—he was very fat. But when he got fitter, he still didn't want to go forward. In fact, the more I pushed him, the slower he got. He would even stop and go into reverse gear. He would back up slowly and persistently until he hit some sort of obstacle. We backed into trees and fences, and once we even fell into a little ditch filled with water. It was hilarious and highly frustrating at the same time. No matter how I used my legs or my whip, he would not go forward. Sometimes he would decide after a while to go anyway, but I was completely at his mercy; on the other hand, I could also have a lot of fun with him. He was the most tolerant, brave and kind pony ever. Often my little sister would join me on his back (without a saddle, of course), and we would go on long trail rides like this. He was awesome, except for this little "I don't want to go forward anymore" thing.

At this time, I didn't have the keys yet to motivate him. Years later, I finally understood how when I met Quimrahil—another very introverted but confident gelding.

Difficulties

The main issue is to get this horse motivated and move forward. This horse seems to be dull and unresponsive, stubborn and resistant. He will buck if you push him, but it is the kind of buck that's easy to stay on; he is too lazy to make big efforts. On top of that, he is very food oriented, so he will go for that patch of nice green grass at every opportunity.

Strong points

This horse is, in general, very reliable and tolerant. He rarely ever spooks, and he keeps his calm in almost every situation. He is easy to get along with and easy to handle in everyday life. And you can get him to do almost anything for a piece of carrot!

Goal

The biggest challenge with this kind of horse is not to increase confidence or to teach him to be braver. He is already brave. Rather, this horse needs to get more responsive and sensitive to aids. The goal of every session should be to end with a motivated horse that wants to put effort into what you ask him to do.

So, what are the keys to get such a horse to put all his heart into what you ask him to do and want to work with you?

Key strategies

1. **Variety is the spice of life.** Nothing is worse for this horse than routine and consistency. Make it interesting! Give your horse variety in your weekly plan. Trail rides, arena work, groundwork, new tasks … get creative to get your horse's interest. This horse will fall asleep if you repeat something too often.
2. **Do less.** Talk less loudly with this horse. Use your legs less. Give smaller signals. Because this horse is non-responsive, we easily fall into the trap of constantly driving them forward with forceful commands. This horse is not deaf, and he can feel a fly landing on his coat. This horse is also not stupid—he knows exactly what you want, but he just doesn't see a lot of sense in moving fast with no reason or incentive. By giving lighter and smaller aids, the horse must listen with more attention.

3. **Keep sessions short.** Have a clear objective. If he can't see the point, he will put in less and less effort. I know it is hard, but quit when he is at his best. Don't give in to the temptation to "ask just one more time" when your horse just put his best effort. He will just tell himself, "I knew it! I will just have to pointlessly repeat this ten times now. I have to save my energy." If you get into a habit of keeping sessions, especially arena sessions, short but progressive, your horse will get into a habit of giving his best effort sooner. In case it happens that you horse gives his best after ten minutes, you can always go on a trail ride.

4. **Ask your horse to do less than he wants to do.** He wants to walk slow, ask him to walk even slower, but keep walking. Soon he will say, "Can't we just walk normally?" Or, if he just stops, you could ask him to back up instead until he says, "Can't we just walk forward?" Make the right thing very easy; make the undesired thing a bit uncomfortable.

5. **Be clear and decisive.** Sometimes you need to be 100 percent clear in what you ask and to follow through to get the desired response. If you fall into the trap of using stronger and stronger aids, you only desensitize your horse and teach him to not respond. If you ask something of this horse, you need to get the horse to do what you asked. But you must do this smartly. If you ask too much too soon, you just get resistance and a bad attitude. Ask for 100 percent effort in little tasks such as a simple halt-walk transition. Build a habit of 100 percent effort in the little requests, and then make your horse feel fantastic about himself and his efforts!

6. **Give incentive.** This horse is constantly asking, "Why should I do this? What is in it for me?" If this horse sees no reason, he will soon quit putting in effort and start to save his energy. You must work a lot with incentive—not bribery but a good reward for when he puts in effort. What kind of reward does your horse like—food, scratches, rest, praise, belly scratch, being allowed to show off his favorite exercise?

7. **Give purpose.** This horse will be at his worst if he sees no reason. Trotting circles in an arena is the worst for this horse. There is just no point. But as soon as he can see a purpose, he will put his heart into it. A trail ride, working cows, pony games, or even a jumping course will give a clear purpose to this horse. My gelding Quimrahil, for example, started to shine when I introduced him to cow work: he suddenly saw a purpose to everything I had taught him before. He loved to show off how well he could push the cow, turn and stop, and he loved that I was so proud of him when he did a good job.

8. **Make a game out of things.** The more you tell this horse what to do or not to do, the more this horse will get resistant. Think about how you can make everything a game with rules, a prize to win and consequences if these rules are not kept. Soon your horse will start to think: "Oh, what can I do to avoid this consequence, and how can I win the prize instead?" Consequence doesn't necessarily mean punishment; for example, it might mean he has to do an extra lap if he avoids taking the jump the first go.

9. **Appreciate his strengths.** This horse might be lazy and low energy, but he is resilient and will almost never spook. You can rely on him. Too often I hear people complain about their introverted horse. I did it too, until I started to value his reliability on trail rides and in difficult situations. In situations when my Arabians would really lose their nerve, Quimrahil would stay calm and centered. Appreciate your horse and stop nagging him about his weaker points.

The introverted/unconfident horse

This horse is sweet, shy and timid. He will not easily express himself. Whereas the previous type of horse rarely wants to go forward out of laziness, this horse can't go forward because he feels so unsure. He retreats into his own little happy world whenever he feels insecure.

Many people call this type of horse unpredictable because we often notice way too late that he is uncertain and push him past his limits. They are very obedient by nature, so they try to please us, even if they are terrified of what we ask them to do. Then, at some point, it becomes just too much and they explode. This is why people think the horse is unpredictable.

Many years ago, I worked with a horse like this. Taram and I were working on his foundation training, but he was scared of everything. He was a timid little flower, trying to be beautiful, but with the slightest wind he would shrink away. He had a hard time going forward under the saddle. All the strategies of the previous horse type would not work for him. He was not interested in food, being more provocative scared him, being firmer and clearer with him just caused him to explode and buck. I spent a lot of time doing nothing much at all with him, just walking next to him with my hand on his neck, talking. Soon Taram started to trust me and to open up. This horse, once I had his trust, gave me all his heart. He was the sweetest, most loving soul. He would never do anything naughty, like the extroverted/confident horses love to do; he just wanted to please me and know that I was happy with him. The more I reassured Taram and the slower I went, the more he opened up and the more he could give. And he would magically be more forward without me needing to push him.

Difficulties

This horse's main problem is trusting you as a teacher and a leader so that he will do what you ask him to do. Whenever he feels scared or overwhelmed, he will shut down and stop "talking." They are hard to read, which is why we so often miss their very subtle signs and run into problems.

The main focus with this horse must be to gain his trust. In general, this horse is not brave. It's not the horse to take into competitions and to jump huge cross-country obstacles because he will easily get scared of energy and speed. He can learn to do these things, but they are not his natural talent.

Strong points

This horse will bond deeply with the human he trusts. If you manage to convince him that you do everything for him and not to him, he will give you his everything. He will be very obedient and rarely ever have a naughty idea. He is gentle and soft, sensitive and willing to please. Oftentimes, he loves dressage because of the safety of repetitive patterns, the closed arena, and "holding hands" through the contact of the reins. This horse likes to be told exactly what to do, how and when because it makes him feel safe.

Goal

The goal for this horse would be to grow in self-confidence so that he is brave enough to come out of his shell. The reason this horse seems to be lazy and non-responsive isn't stubbornness, but a lack of confidence. This means that if you get this horse to be more confident in himself, in communicating with you, and in his environment, the problems will disappear.

Key strategies

1. **Go slow.** Don't rush anything with this horse. Think about how you can break everything down into mini steps. This horse isn't stupid, but he's very scared of not doing things right. So, if he doesn't understand 100 percent because you skipped a mini step, he will get worried. This doesn't mean that you can only walk with this horse at a snail's speed; it mainly means that you slow your energy down. This horse is extremely good in feeling our vibes, so if you pretend to be patient but inside you are a nuclear reactor, you shouldn't be surprised that this horse has trouble trusting you. Therefore, whenever things start to go wrong, slow down. Stop, breathe, and think how you could explain better. Have an attitude of patience and things will go a lot faster with this horse.

2. **Repetition.** Repeat until he does it by himself; then you know he gets it. This horse loves to show you how well he can do things if you let him. Repetitions make him feel safe that he is doing the right thing. Repeating also gives him the opportunity to settle and feel okay with an exercise. In general, with this horse you can't repeat too often. It's the perfect horse for perfectionists. With each repetition he will do things better, he will be more awake, more with you, more involved. But at the same time, just don't criticize him when he doesn't manage something perfectly. Adding pressure when things go wrong is absolutely the wrong way to go with this horse.

3. **Reassure him a lot.** His biggest fear is doing things wrong, so let him know that everything is fine. Give praise when you see him trying, not only when he manages to execute all the way, through your voice, a soft rub, smiling, which all work wonders with this horse. Do everything you can to send your loving vibes to this horse.

4. **Build confidence.** This will build up this horse's confidence in you and in his ability to do the right thing, especially in the beginning stages of your relationship with this horse. This horse might be

afraid or unsure about a lot of things: vet, farrier, clipper, shower, leaving the herd … anything new. Take time to get these things right. It's easy to manage this horse through these procedures because he is so obedient. But he will never be really relaxed. Take the time to explain your horse that he really has nothing to fear, and show him how to relax emotionally and physically with these basic tasks. For this, you need to learn to read him.

5. **Read your horse's subtle signs.** Get good reading your horse's subtle signs, especially facial expressions. If he stops blinking, this is usually the first indicator that he is worried. Watch out for wrinkles above or under the eye. Watch the lips, are they tight? When moving, watch your horses back: Is it loose or tight? Is his neck just a little up or is it relaxed? The signs are very subtle, so you must observe your horse and learn to know how he communicates. Make a list of the signs when he relaxes and feels good and of the signs he gives when he is worried.

6. **Wait for the lick and chew.** Licking and chewing are sure signs that the horse is relaxing. And this is what you want with this horse in particular. You want to make sure your horse licked and chewed during the exercise. If you do several tasks in a row and didn't allow your horse enough time to "think," you risk building his tension and either a shutdown or explosion. If you keep pushing him on, you risk an explosion, so just stop, wait for the lick and chew, and try again.

7. **Be a certain-but-soft leader.** It is easy to get hung up in being too soft and waiting too much for this horse. But even this horse needs a leader who knows what to do and who believes in him that he can actually do it. Saying to your horse, "Let's do this" in a calm way is better than the less confident, "Can you do this?" Can you radiate confidence that your horse is capable of overcoming his fears? Be soft but certain and have a plan.

8. **Whisper to this horse.** This horse is very sensitive. Even if he doesn't always move off with the speed of light like the extroverted types, you will see that he reacts immediately in some way. With

this horse, you can whisper and talk very softly. In fact, he will get scared if you show big gestures, speak loudly, or increase the phases too quickly. What is just firm enough for a confident type of horse would be upsetting for this horse, but once this horse understands, you can move him around with the touch of a fly.

9. **Spend undemanding time.** One of the best ways to gain this horse's confidence and trust is to just spend time without expecting anything. Don't even expect him to sniff you! Really: NO EXPECTATIONS! As soon as you expect something, even if it is unconscious in your mind, this horse might feel it as pressure. If you regularly just spend time, hang out in the field or in his stall, he will get confident with your presence. Eventually, he will start to make contact with you. Then you can start to offer soft scratches (yes, this is the horse that likes soft scratches and rubs), and slowly he will start to enjoy your company. Take the time to become friends. Establish a heart-to-heart connection. This will be the horse that can literally read your thoughts.

10. **Reward this horse when he shows initiative.** This horse's biggest fear is doing something wrong and being told off. This is a reason why this horse is so obedient. In a way this horse lacks self-confidence and boldness. He is almost too reserved and too obedient. So, the day this horse has an idea or a proposition to do something, take it! Praise him! This is a sign that he is confident enough to express himself towards you. I once trained a very sweet but very timid gelding. The day he searched my jacket and actually nibbled on it, I was so happy because he was finally confident enough to "invade" my space like that. If it gets too much, it is really not a problem to say to this horse, "That's enough now." Reward courage, boldness and self-confidence when they express their opinion.

Your goal: a centered horse

With a well-trained horse, it will be hard to tell what type of personality he is. If you use the strategies consistently, your horse will even out. He will become willing, motivated, calm and trusting. Every horse has its little flaws; the question is, are you evening them out with your training or are you highlighting them with your training? With good training, your horse should become more and more centered until he is the "perfect" horse.

These are the pillars of good horse training: being able to adapt to every type of horse and being humble enough to completely change style and approach so that it fits a particular horse in a particular situation.

What type of horse fits you?

Reading this, you probably already thought here and there, "Oh, I would like that horse" or "That one wouldn't fit me so well." Not everybody clicks with the same type of horse. Having a bad fit with your horse can be very difficult. Sometimes it just doesn't fit, and it is better to find a better fit for the horse and for you. So, if you already have a horse, I hope that you get some clues out of this to make your partnership work even better. If you are looking into buying a horse, now you can learn to evaluate upfront which type would suit you best.

I meet so many people who bought themselves the "Dream Horse." The black stallion, the white exuberant Arabian, the reliable draft horse, but then they bring the horse to me for urgent retraining. Sometimes the horse of your dreams is not the animal you can live your horse-dream with.

So, what personality do you have? Are you a bold and confident person and rider or are you more careful and like to practice details? Do you just like to relax on quiet trail rides, or would you love to do show jumping against the clock?

If you are bold and extroverted yourself, probably you would get very annoyed and bored with the introverted types of horses. You would scare the unconfident type, and you would be frustrated with the confident introverted type because he just doesn't love speed!

If you are a more introverted and unconfident person, you will get very scared with the confident/extroverted type. He has way too much energy and too many own ideas for you. He needs a leader who matches his energy and enthusiasm, and if you can't bring that up because you are just not like that, he will take over and make his own plans.

If you are a laid-back, confident rider and you have this crazy extroverted scared horse who needs to run a lot, you would probably get frustrated. It won't be possible to enjoy quiet trail rides in nature because they will always end up being pretty fast and hectic. You would fit better with the introverted types.

If you are an extroverted but rather emotional rider, you probably wouldn't fit at all with the unconfident/extroverted type. You would scare each other. There would be no one who can give confidence to the other and be the leader. You would probably be best with the confident/introverted type who is quiet and reliable.

If you love speed and aren't bothered by the occasional crazy attack, you will love the extroverted/unconfident type. These horses are obedient (when they aren't scared) and are never tired. Become their trusted leader, and they will give you everything.

If you would love to have a horse your kids can also ride, definitely choose an introverted horse. Unconfident ones will be more obedient and sweeter. Confident ones will be more tolerant, but the kids will have a harder time getting the horse to move (and the occasional buck will be in the program).

HORSE YOU	Extrovert/ Confident	Extrovert/ Unconfident	Introvert/ Confident	Introvert/ Unconfident
Extrovert/ Confident	Perfect fit!	Good fit	You will get bored or learn to wake him up	Your energy will overwhelm this horse
Extrovert/ Emotional	Possible fit if you are a confident rider	Not ideal	Perfect fit!	Not ideal
Laid back	Bad fit: Horse will be bored with you	Good fit: you will calm the horse	Okay, if you learn to motivate the horse	Good fit
Timid/Quiet	Not ideal	Not ideal	Perfect fit!	Good fit
Kids	Good fit for kids with some riding experience	Not safe	Perfect fit!	Good fit, if the horse is well trained

How to test temperament and character of a young horse

With young horses who are not matured yet in their character and temperament, it can be very hard to tell what kind of personality they will have later on. A lot is still open to change because it is not just genetics that play a role; upbringing and environment have a huge influence.

Nevertheless, you can make some assessment based on the following:

- **Reaction to novelties:** Bring an umbrella or a tarp in the horse's field and see what he does. Is he curious or does he wait for others to check it out first? How long does it take for him to check it out?

- **Reaction to being alone:** How does he react when he leaves the herd or if the horse in the neighboring stall leaves? Is he very gregarious?
- **Reaction to new environment:** How does he react when you take him for a walk somewhere he doesn't know? Does he want to turn around and hide behind you or does he walk in front, eager to explore?
- **Reaction to restriction:** How does he react when you hold him tight and restrict his movement? How does he react when you hold his head? Does he get nervous or does he not care?
- **General sensitivity to touch and pressure:** How easily can you push him around? How sensitive is he when you touch his hair, his leg, etc.?

Even with the best training, you can't change your horse's innate character. But you can help your horse be his best and grow past his fears and anxieties. Every horse brings his own trouble, but it's up to you to decide with which kind of trouble you can deal with best.

Remember, these are only guidelines. You don't want to fall into the trap of putting your horse into a fixed category. Often people ask me, "What type is my horse?" and I reply, "Your horse is your horse." By this I mean that he/she has his/her unique personality. There will be tendencies for sure, but every horse has his own personality. You must learn to not only read him but also adapt and change as necessary. Don't keep doing something that's not working just because somebody said, "Your horse is this personality, so you should treat him like this or that." Your horse will change as the situation changes, the day changes, the season changes, the education progresses, and your relationship progresses. Use this knowledge to your advantage by using all of it, not just what is written in one category.

Exercise:
Which personality fits your horse?
Which fits you?

Visit chapter 7 in the workbook. The questions provided will help you find out your horse's personality and how it matches with yours.

If you haven't downloaded the workbook yet, you can get it here: https://www.understandingisthekey.com/workbook

Alternatively, make a list in your journal of your horse's main personality traits and another list for your traits. Of the four personalities described in this chapter, which one fits your horse best? Which fits you best? Do you match? If you don't match, what can you do to untangle the mismatch? Are you willing to put in the extra work and effort to grow as much as necessary?

A Horse's Natural Needs

A happy horse starts with fulfilling his natural needs. The best training in the world can't make a horse happy if his essential needs aren't satisfied. I feel a bit ridiculous talking about this topic because I know that horse lovers give the well-being of their beloved equine friend a lot of thought. But during the last few years working as a professional, I have seen so many weird things happen between owner and horse that I feel this topic needs to be addressed to make this book complete.

To give you an example, let me tell you a little story. A woman rang me up one day. The little four-year-old Welsh pony gelding, Erowan, whom she had bought for her four-year-old daughter, wasn't behaving at all. He was running into people, biting, not standing still for grooming and acting aggressively when feeding. When they took him for a walk with the daughter, all he did was drag them to the next patch of grass. He was a true pony: a brat, a nightmare and not at all safe for the girl. On top of that, he had a hay allergy, so he was coughing all the time.

I asked the lady how the pony was kept. She told me that they had him stabled since a few months because the field was so muddy. He would be more comfortable in a clean stall with a big bed of straw. I asked her if he had some company. The answer was no, because he was playing so hard with the other horses that they were worried about his health. Even when he was allowed out on the paddock for a few short hours, he went alone. He was a young pony with a very high play drive, and his energy had to vent somehow.

Why was this pony acting up? The owner saw no reason for the horse to be unhappy as he lived in a comfortable stall with a big bed of straw and without other horses pestering him. Essentially, though, it was like locking up a highly energetic twelve-year-old boy in a toilet cubicle. What can you expect?

Too often we project our human needs and feelings onto our horses. Anthropomorphism is counterproductive when training horses, but it's not helpful when it comes to keeping a horse either. Horses are evolved to live in big open spaces, while humans evolved living in caves. As humans, we tend have a strong urge to make our horses comfortable, cozy, happy, and feeling well. There is no blame; I am in the same boat. I love to buy stuff for my horses and then put it to use. I have more rugs than horses, I love food supplements, and to try all kinds of lotions and potions. But do these things actually make our horses happy or just us?

Horses' general needs

Company: Horses are herd animals

Horses need equine company. Horses will only feel safe when being with other equines in a herd. They are stronger together and able to see more danger. Horses will only rest when they feel 100 percent safe and know that a friend is watching out for danger in the meantime. Horses are highly social and will build lasting friendships, just like us. They need social interaction, mutual grooming, playing and grazing together to feel content and happy.

Once I saw on Facebook a lady asking for advice about accommodating a weanling. Her question was about which option was best:

- Option A: in a yard with goose
- Option B: a bigger field but only with chickens
- Option C: a very big field, close to the house, but no company, although the foal would be able see the goose from afar

I didn't know what to say. It would have been funny if it had been a joke, but this was a serious question. Horses need *equine* company. Geese, chicken, and sheep are not equivalent! Yes, horses can adapt because their genetic programming makes sure they survive, but will the horse be really happy and feel safe? Probably not.

Grass and roughage: Horses are herbivores

The horse's digestive tract is designed to deal with a constant flow of food. The main means of digestion is bacterial fermentation. Stomach acid is produced all the time, and food passes rapidly through the stomach. This means that if a horse runs without food for longer than four hours, the stomach will be empty and the acid will burn the stomach lining. Being able to constantly nibble on some sort of roughage ensures that the horse's digestive tract stays healthy.

Constant movement: Horses are steppe animals

Horses need to move. In nature they will be on the move for long periods of the day looking for the next patch of grass. This constant movement keeps their joints and legs healthy, their digestion tract going, and their muscles ready to run. An Australian study of distances traveled by feral horses in the outback showed that they average 15 km per day.[10] Movement is what keeps a horse fit and healthy, in body and mind. Restrict a horse's movement, and you will provoke a host of problems ranging from stereotypic behaviors, digestive issues, and what is called "soundness."

Space: Horses want to see and move

Ideally, the horse should have enough space to go for a good gallop. A small square field is better than nothing, but will not satisfy a horse's need to walk, run, travel and observe the surroundings. Horses hate restrictions, because it means being trapped and not being able to escape from danger.

Routine: Horses are creatures of habit

Horses appreciate a regular routine of eating, resting, working, grooming and playing. Routines make horses feel safe. Anything out of the norm gives them reason to worry.

Mental stimulation: Horses hate to be bored

Horses like to be active, not just physically but mentally. In nature they have to think about where to find food, water, and a place to rest. We take all this away from them if we keep them stabled with limited turnout. It's boring to be enclosed in square walls or fences all day long.

Leadership: Horses like hierarchy

Horses are evolved to live in a hierarchical structure. In order to feel comfortable and safe, they need a confident leader they trust.

Your domestic horse's needs

Clean living conditions

Hygiene is vital for our horse's health. Unless one owns several square miles where horses can roam freely, it's imperative for their well-being to keep everything neat and clean. Hoof health, respiratory health, and parasite control are directly connected with keeping the horse's living conditions clean. This means work because horses are poop machines. To keep a horse on deep wet bedding, deep mud, or a pasture covered in poop is seriously detrimental to his health, and he will run up your vet's bill over time.

Keeping the stable nice and clean and clearing up the paddock regularly should be the norm.

Company and social contact

As stated above, horses need equine company. Of course, the horse will make friends with other animals, such as a goat, if there is no other horse around. But a horse and goat can't groom mutually, communicate the same way, and a horse can't feed the same way with non-equine friends. Young horses in particular also depend on other horses to learn correct social behaviors and rules.

I once worked with a four-year-old trotting mare, Esperance. She was raised with a bottle after her mother died while giving birth. Unfortunately, during the first few months of her life, she was only with people and had no contact with other horses. Even though she was put with other horses at five months old, she never caught up. She considered humans as her herd and was afraid of other horses. As a consequence, training her was pretty difficult because she never learned to talk "horse." She was a socially disturbed horse, unable to live a normal horse life and unable to fully understand either human or horse.

Horses need equine company. This is the most important happy-factor for your horse.

Constant foraging

Make some sort of forage available to your horse at all times. Don't let your horse go without any sort of foraging for longer than four hours. Feeding high-energy meals might satisfy nutrient and energy needs of your horse, but not his need to constantly nibble and chew.

Horses need to chew about 55,000 times so that their brain signals they have had enough. Think about how you can provide foraging opportunities for your horse if he is not turned out in a field, especially if he needs to be on a diet. Hay nets or other slow feeders are a great option, and they remove the risk that the horse will overeat.

Hoof care

Domestic horses need regular hoof care, even if they are kept outside in big pastures twenty-four-seven and are barefoot. By regular, I mean that they need to be trimmed every four to eight weeks, depending on growth, hoof use, and overall quality of the hoof. No need to wait until the hooves look ugly. The more you expect from your horse, the closer you need to pay attention. Become knowledgeable about this so that you can stay independent to a certain degree of your hoof-care provider. Take responsibility for your horses' hooves; they are crucial to your horses' long-term soundness and performance.

Selective breeding over the last century left many horses with dysfunctional feet. Returning to a more natural lifestyle can do wonders for weak hooves, but they need to be looked after. A regular trim schedule is a must for optimal health and performance. I am pro-barefoot, but if the horse is sore and his feet don't support him, he needs protection! If necessary, protect the hooves with hoof boots, glue-ons, or iron shoes. Please, don't leave your horse barefoot for the sake of barefoot if he is sore!

Vet care and vaccinations

To avoid epidemic outbreaks of illnesses that might threaten your horse's life, vaccinate your horse. Every country has different regulations, so speak to your vet to establish a vaccination plan suitable for your region. Hopefully, you will only need a yearly shot. Make the effort to find a good horse-experienced vet that can address all the odd health questions that come up.

Parasite control

Horses are evolved to always have a certain number of worms, and it is perfectly normal for wild horses to have parasites. But our domestic horses live in much smaller spaces, and sometimes they just can't avoid eating close to their own droppings. A good parasite control plan is an absolute must for any horse. Unfortunately, parasites start to be resistant to treatments available on the market, but selective deworming helps avoid these resistances to build-up. Essentially it works like this:

- Every three months (two months for foals up to two years), take a poop sample and have an egg count performed. For this, you either ask your vet or send it to a lab that offers this service.
- The result of the test will tell you if your horse needs to get dewormed or not. Up to a certain worm/egg count, the horse doesn't need deworming.
- If you have a whole herd, you will find that it's always the same horses who have a slightly higher worm count. You will only need to treat horses with an elevated worm count.

- Ideally, you redo the egg count about ten days after deworming—this allows you to check whether the worms are resistant to the treatment you used.

Selective deworming has many benefits besides avoiding the resistance of the parasites to build up. It also helps you save money on expensive wormer, as most horses don't even need to be wormed four times a year and therefore preserve the horse's intestinal flora. Pay attention though, certain worms won't be visible in the worm count. For those you will need to do more specific test. Ask your vet.

At the stable where I have worked for years, we use this protocol. Seventy-five percent of the horses only needed one wormer per year, 20 percent needed two wormers, and only 5 percent needed three or four wormers.

Shelter

Horses need to have shelter in extreme conditions, such as heat, rain, snow, wind or hail. Horses can be very resistant to poor conditions, but selective breeding caused many breeds to be way more sensitive. There is a big difference in terms of resistance when you compare a Haflinger to a Quarter horse or a thoroughbred.

If you keep your horse outside and don't bring it in every night, you should provide a shelter that is closed on three sides for your horse. In some countries it is even a legal obligation to have a shelter available in the field, and natural shelter, like trees and bushes, are not considered sufficient. In summer, natural shelter provides enough protection, but not in winter when the leaves are gone.

Mental stimulation

Horses like to be mentally active. Making everything as comfortable as possible for them makes life boring. Housing concepts such as "Paddock Paradise" or the German "Hit Active Stable" provide mental stimulation for the horse. Food is found on different places at random times, but not all the time. As a consequence, horses are able to imitate nature and walk around looking for food a lot more. Think about how you can make daily life more interesting for your horse. Hanging hay nets at different places is a very easy way to change routines. Separate the horses' shelter, water troughs, and feeding areas as much as possible so that your horse is motivated to move from one place to the other.

The other part of mental stimulation is the time your horse spends with you. In my experience, horses are more content if they have their "own" human and regular "work" or activity—both physical work and mental work. Learning new things contributes to a horse's happiness, big time.

Consequences of not fulfilling needs

When you fail to fulfill these basic needs, there are many negative consequences.

Stereotypic behaviors

Stereotypy is a ritualistic or repetitive movement and, in horses, it includes behaviors such as weaving, cribbing, wind sucking, and stall walking. So many stable-kept horses suffer from these behaviors. The horse doesn't see these behaviors as a problem or stressful; for them, the behaviors are a way of dealing with confinement and other stresses.

Each time the horse performs one of these stereotypic behaviors, he will receive a hit of endorphins. This makes the horse feel better for a moment because endorphins are the feel-good hormones of the body, and as a result, the horse becomes addicted to the behavior. It's much like eating chocolate for us humans—but just as eating lots of chocolate isn't great for our bodies, so these stereotypic behaviors in horses can lead to serious health issues.

Aggression towards people and other horses

This problem mostly comes up due to lack of social contact and boredom: not enough exercise, not enough mental stimulation, and lack of good training, not enough foraging, and having an empty stomach for too long.

Depression

Where some horses turn aggressive, the more introverted counterparts become depressed. Confinement and isolation are the biggest causes of depression.

Behavioral issues

If a horse can't play with other horses, he will try to play with you. The confident/extroverted type of horse will especially start to be overly playful or "disrespectful" if he doesn't have the opportunity to play and run in a field. The energy just has to come out!

Leg problems

Long periods of standing still in a stable, deep bedding, sudden work, and the wrong use of leg protection can cause serious problems for the horse's joints, tendons and bones. The horse is designed to stay in movement. Long periods of rest cause the synovia in the joints to become thicker and less lubricated, and when the horse is then turned out into a field and immediately runs and bucks because he is happy, this can lead to serious damage.

Hoof problems

No hoof, no horse. If the horse's hoof isn't healthy, the horse can't be sound. Hoof problems will cascade on all parts of the horse's body because as soon as a horse starts to compensate for the discomfort in his feet, other problems follow.

The first reason for hoof problems is a lack of hygiene. As discussed previously, deep bedding, mud, and walking in excrement is detrimental for hoof health. The second reason is lack of movement: no movement, no stimulation for growth, no internal foot development. The third reason is inadequate nutrition, i.e., food that's too rich, too many carbohydrates, and mineral imbalance. Educate yourself to be able to make independent and informed decisions for your horse.

Digestive problems

Long periods of no food intake, high grain meals, and little roughage, combined with the stress of confinement and too little movement very quickly leads to ulcers and colic in domestic horses. One very simple way to help would be to provide roughage twenty-four-seven in a slow feeder or hay net.

Respiratory problems

Damp, warm, and dusty stables can cause respiratory problems in horses. Moldy hay and wet bedding additionally irritate the sensitive airways of the horse. Allergic cough, COPD (Chronic Obstructive Pulmonary Disease), and being sensitive to infections are very common problems among stabled horses. Open the windows and doors, let the air in, keep the bedding clean, and only feed them clean hay. Or allow your horse to live outside.

Too much energy

Many horses who only see their box, their little field, the walker, and the arena will be excessively reactive. Everything seems to spook them. As they never get to see anything, they never get the opportunity to learn.

Training and everyday life can be made so much easier with our horses if we fulfill their need for company, movement, space, and forage. Vet bills and food costs can be greatly reduced if we keep our horses more like nature intended.

I love seeing the trend toward more natural horse keeping during the last ten years. More and more horse lovers are discovering the advantages of keeping their horse outside in a herd. Unfortunately, the way we have selectively bred our horses over generations has made them more frail and less resistant than they once were, so we have to find a healthy balance between wrapping them in cotton wool and letting them live naturally.

Exercise:
How can you support your horse's ideal living conditions?

We must find a balance between our own resources (time, space, money) and what our horse would need. I believe that every horse owner acts out of best interest for his/her horse. However, the more educated we are and the more we reject anthropomorphism, the better we will be able to take care of our horses.

Go to chapter 8 in the workbook. Use the provided questions to examine your horse's living conditions. These will help you uncover straightforward ways to make his life happier.

If you haven't downloaded the workbook yet, you can get it here: https://www.understandingisthekey.com/workbook

Alternatively, take your journal and reflect on your horse's current living conditions. How far or close are you to offering them the ideal living situation? Which simple things can you do to meet your horse's needs and provide him with a happier life? Could you provide him hay in a hay net so that he has less time without any roughage? How can you make sure that he has more social contact and more movement? How could you create cleaner living conditions for your horse?

Part 3:

Understand the Journey

Finally, you are going to lead your horse down a certain path towards one goal: To create a reliable and competent partner who is easy and fun to ride and, even better, loves to spend time with you. What is the order of tasks your horse has to learn? How can you create this relationship you always dreamt of having? Let's dive deep.

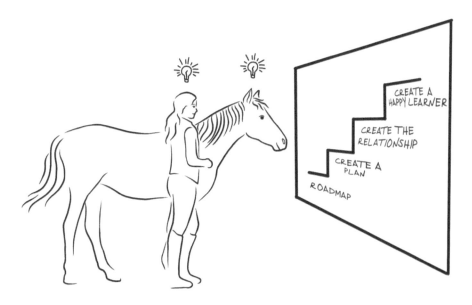

From Foal to Dream Horse

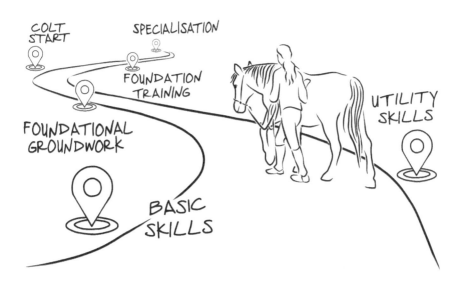

COLT
START

SPECIALISATION

FOUNDATION
TRAINING

FOUNDATIONAL
GROUNDWORK

UTILITY
SKILLS

BASIC
SKILLS

E very horse owner ultimately wants to have a confident and willing horse that is easy to handle in everyday life and is a pleasure to ride.

Very often we only start to think about how to reach that goal seriously, once we meet a horse that wasn't such a pleasure to ride or to handle. Or both. It's quite frustrating (and sometimes painful) to deal with a horse that has some holes in his education and foundation.

It's very much like when you try to save time and money when building a house. One might be tempted to be sloppy in the foundation (because you can't see it anyway), but without the foundation, the house won't stand solid and strong and the first cracks will soon show.

Everything you have read until now will help you apply what you will learn in this chapter. This whole book is a roadmap to help you to develop your youngster into your dream horse, and developing a dream horse is mostly a matter of attitude, awareness, and solid knowledge and only secondary about correct techniques. Knowledge about the horses' nature, how they learn, what they need to be happy, how to read their body language. It's about your ability to make a plan, to be structured and, most importantly, to be disciplined to do the work required and keep going no matter what.

This chapter will give you the piece of the puzzle you were waiting for— the actual tasks. All the little things a horse must know in order to be the dream horse that is confident and willing and a pleasure to ride. I will outline what a horse has to learn in what order from two perspectives:

- **Skill-based order:** starting at the basics all the way through foundation training
- **Chronological order:** starting on day one of the horse's life

This will give you important guidelines whether you have a little foal or your horse is already three years old.

Skill-based roadmap

There is a logical order of how any horse should learn all the necessary skills. These skills can be grouped into four main categories:

- Basic skills
- Foundational groundwork
- Colt start
- Foundation training

Only after this basic training should a horse enter specialization training according to the discipline you choose, which is beyond the scope of this book.

Today's reality is that horses barely learn the basic skills. They are rushed through their colt start and enter specialization training too soon—all for the sake of fast results, to be successful sooner, to make money, and because we are impatient to get to the fancy stuff. The result is too often a horse that is not the easiest to handle in everyday life—a horse that is confused and can't handle anything out of the norm.

Don't skip the basics. You will fall in love with the process and with teaching your horse everything step by step. There comes an immense feeling of gratification and fulfillment watching your own horse grow in his confidence and competence, and knowing it was you who taught your horse.

Whenever I get a new horse with unknown history, I first check where the horse is along this roadmap. If I find holes in the basics, I will fix them first before advancing to any other task.

The basic skills

The basic skills build the foundation of a healthy and comfortable daily relationship with our horses. The skills consist of three main categories: socializing with humans and horses, daily handling, and utility skills (vet, farrier, transport).

1. Socializing with humans and horses

Do you remember the story of Esperance, the mare who was raised with a bottle? When I got her to start her under saddle, I tried to add her to one of my herds as she would stay for longer with me. But she would just not settle into the herd. We tried for about four weeks, but she showed no interest in other horses and was even afraid of them, although they weren't bad to her. She was stressed and losing weight, and she started to be quite unhappy.

When I started working with her, I discovered huge gaps in her basic relationship with people. She was very confident, but she had no idea how to communicate in a respectful manner, attacking me whenever I made my boundaries clear and didn't back down. She had not been socialized well, not with horses or with people.

I had to catch up a lot with this mare before I could actually start her under saddle. This very first step is so important. If a horse is not well socialized, lacks confidence or respect in its relationship with people, any training will be more difficult and time-consuming.

2. Daily handling

Daily handling tasks any horse should be able to do with ease and confidence:

- Catching
- Haltering
- Tying
- Respect at feeding time
- Picking up the feet
- Grooming
- Touching all over, also ears, belly, mouth, under the tail
- Leading with respect
- Yielding to pressure on a basic level
- Accepting the worm paste
- Going for walks
- Confrontation with unknown and strange objects

3. Utility skills

Teaching these skills usually takes a bit more time and practice, but they are absolutely essential for daily life without worries:

- Showering
- Trailer loading
- Being alone
- Needle preps
- Bandaging legs
- Taking temperature
- Treating wounds
- Clipping

- Standing still without being tied
- Using fly spray
- Eye rinsing
- Placing the hoof on hoof stand
- Holding the hoof up for longer periods of time
- Having feet handled by an unknown person

Think of teaching your horse how to handle the strange human world when teaching the basic skills. Nothing we do with our horses comes naturally to them. Take the time and effort to teach and explain everything to your horse. This will be the strong foundation that all else will be built on.

Foundational groundwork

A solid foundation for riding starts on the ground. Through groundwork we can show and explain to our horses how to be soft and yielding to any kind of pressure, which will later help the horse to understand the rider's aids better. We can teach the horse to be confident when facing scary situations, and we can teach our horse to have good impulsion. The better a horse's foundation is on the ground, the easier his start under saddle will be later. Every single minute you spend with your youngster practicing ground skills is well-invested time.

When doing groundwork with a young horse, think in these categories:

1. Establish communication and language.
2. Gain your horse's willingness to give you control over his gaits.
3. Gain your horse's willingness to give you control over his direction.
4. Boost your horse's confidence to accept the rider and to handle stressful situations
5. Prepare your horse physically to carry a rider.

I started my own mare, Salimah, only when she was already eight years old. She was a broodmare until I bought her. Her basic handling skills were okay, but she was very explosive and emotional as soon as it was about working in an arena or being alone. She basically didn't know how to communicate with me, and this was the main reason for her being so emotional.

I knew that if I got on her back before we were able to have a dialogue and before she was confident with me controlling her gait and direction, I would be in real danger. I didn't want to be on her when she had one of her emotional outbreaks, for sure! It took about four weeks to prepare her well on the ground. Then her start was easy. She had learned how to "talk" to me and be confident with the fact that I control gait and direction.

Problems when starting a horse only come up when the horse wasn't properly prepared, go too fast or skip steps. During the colt start we ask the horse to accept three things, which are completely against his nature as a prey animal:

1. A predator is sitting on his back with a saddle and a cinch, which is tightening around his rib cage.
2. He must give up control over the direction he wants to go.
3. He must give up control over the gait or speed he wants to travel in.

If these things are not well explained to the horse, he will most likely become afraid and show some sort of defensive behaviors. Bucking and bolting, fear and worry are just not helpful when starting a horse.

By giving a horse a good foundation on the ground, I can effectively prepare him to understand the process of being started more easily and with less stress. The start under saddle should be a positive experience for the horse, and it begins long before I ever ride the horse for the first time. In the end, the start is not just something in a horse's life; it will color its perception of the rider for the rest of his life.

A horse will have a good foundation on the ground if you can do the following exercises:

1. Establish communication and language
   - Yielding to rhythmic pressure: Backing up, yielding shoulders, yielding hind quarters, going forward and stopping.
   - Touch-it game: The horse is sent to an object and asked to touch it. This builds communication between the horse and trainer.
   - Trail obstacles: Send the horse over easy obstacles, such as a tarp, ground poles, a pedestal, a seesaw. This builds courage and communication.
2. Gain your horse's willingness to give you control over his gaits
   - Circle left and right, maintain gait for two to four laps without correction
   - Up and downwards transitions when circling
   - Yielding backwards to steady pressure
   - Lateral flexion
3. Gain your horse's willingness to give you control over his direction
   - Send horse around two markers in a figure of eight at walk and trot
   - Yielding the shoulders to steady pressure
   - Yielding the hindquarters to steady pressure
   - Yielding sideways with a fence and without a fence

4. Boost your horse's confidence to accept the rider
   - Toss stick and string over horse's back and hindquarters
   - Shake flag all around your horse
   - Bounce a big ball around horse
   - Put a ball on his back
   - Come to the mounting block

5. Prepare your horse physically to carry a rider
   - Ground poles at walk and trot
   - Go for long walks, jogging
   - Gymnastic free-jumping
   - Teach your horse to work in a forward down outline (without gadgets)
   - Work on hills

These tasks will help me to develop certain mental and emotional qualities. I want to create a horse that is connected to me, calm, and confident in what I am asking him to do. These are way more important qualities than executing the exercises to perfection but with a poor attitude.

The colt start

By now your horse is well socialized, has good manners in everyday life, has a solid foundation in groundwork, and is ready to be started under saddle. Where do you start, how do you go about it?

The secret of a good, uneventful colt start is not to have an easy horse. The secret lies in being able to break down every single step into mini steps that are easily understood by the horse. As soon as you try to go fancy and fast, you will rush the horse and that's where the trouble starts. A horse doesn't need to be broken in; you can work just as well with your horse and help him understand all the new challenges. Time and patience go a long way when starting a horse. Horses are very willing by nature to be trained, especially if you took the time beforehand to create a relationship of mutual trust and respect.

A few summers ago, I received a two-year-old Irish Cob filly named Eleven to educate. She had become way taller and stronger than the owner hoped for. As it so often happens with two-year-olds, Eleven discovered how strong she was and became difficult to handle—pushy and invasive. I had her for two months. During this time, I refined all the necessary basic and utility skills and gave her a solid foundation on the ground, keeping in mind that she would need to be started the following year.

One year later, the owners brought her back for me to start her under saddle. During the first session, I just checked what the now three-year-old filly remembered from the year before. Amazingly, it was as if the last session had been the day before, not more than one year ago! She was so responsive, confident, and eager to please that it was a pleasure working with her again. I was able to go through all five stages of the colt start much quicker than usual. On ride number four, we went on our first trail ride alone. Because she had a solid foundation on the ground, she progressed so much faster and remained calm and confident throughout the process.

Starting a horse takes skill. Please take your horse to a trainer if you feel you don't possess the necessary skill. I know that it is the dream of many horse owners to start their youngster themselves; this is such an important moment in your horse's life, you don't want anything going wrong. Take the right decisions and get competent support or bring your horse to a trainer you trust and who shares your values.

A colt start consists of five stages:

- Accept the cinch
- Accept the saddle
- Accept the rider
- Accept and respect the directions of the rider
- Accept and understand the bit (if wanted)

1. Accept the cinch

A horse doesn't need to buck when he learns to accept the cinch. However, horses (as previously discussed) are claustrophobic by nature, which is why so many horses react with bucking when cinched up for the first time. Break this step down as much as possible and go slowly. Start with just using an elastic surcingle, usually used to hold a light blanket in place, and progress to using a lunging cinch or a bareback pad. Cinch up slowly and progressively, always moving your horse's feet a bit between each cinching.

You simply can't know how your horse will react, so do it in a safe environment, such as a round pen. Use frequent disengaging of the hindquarters to relax the horse. Don't chase your horse out on the circle to "buck it out"! Go slow and let him experience the fact that the cinch isn't scary and doesn't harm him.

My goal is that the horse can perform all foundational groundwork exercises well while wearing a cinch because it shows me that the horse accepted and relaxed wearing the cinch.

2. Accept the saddle

Wearing a saddle can make a big difference to some horses than wearing only a cinch. A saddle moves, and so the horse can see the flaps moving as he trots and canters. The stirrups are bouncing against the ribcage. These two factors can worry some horses a lot.

The goal is that the horse can trot, canter, and take a little jump wearing the saddle without getting tight and without bucking.

The horse should relax when wearing a saddle. Only then will the horse be ready for the next step.

3. Accept the rider

This is THE most important step when starting a horse. A horse has to be 100 percent confident in the rider on his back. Even if the horse has just a tiny doubt, this will amplify his reactions whenever you find yourself in a difficult situation. Your horse needs to be totally relaxed about having you on his back.

If the horse doesn't stand still at the mounting block when I want to get on, I know that I am missing confidence. The goal, therefore, is that the horse positions himself at the mounting block and waits patiently for me to get on and checks in with me, bending left or right afterwards. He is connected and relaxed when he carries the head low and continuously blinks his eyes.

Once I achieved this step, I can help the horse accept me as a passenger at a walk and trot. Note that I wrote *passenger*—I don't give any major directions yet. The goal is for the horse to find forward and to find back his natural balance with the weight of the rider. Most horses have a hard time to find forward during the first rides. The horse simply must discover that he can still move normally with the rider on his back.

I can do this either with an assistant on the ground who lunges the horse, or on my own while riding in a round pen or a small arena. Sometimes I will also ask a friend to ride with a calm horse in front. My goal is that I feel the horse walking and trotting freely and in a relaxed manner.

During this stage, I want to check the following tasks off my list:

- Lateral flexion
- Backing up
- Taking a trot from a smooch and light tap on the rear or shoulders
- Disengaging the hindquarters
- Walk-to-trot transitions
- Slow to a stop when I relax

4. Accept and respect directions

Once the horse has found forward and understood that he can walk and trot with the rider, he is ready to learn about directions. Now it is time to transfer all the preparatory exercises about gait and direction in the saddle.

Essentially the horse learns two things:

- To follow my energy
- To follow my focus

Now he has to learn to understand and follow my directions more precisely: stop and go, left and right.

My goal in this step is to ride the horse in all three gaits. The horse should respond willingly when I ask him to go forward and come to a gentle stop when I relax and quit riding. The horse should turn willingly left and right in all three gaits. During this stage, I want to check the following tasks off my list.

> *"Follow my energy" always has priority over "follow my focus." I always make sure that I can ask my horse to speed up and to slow down before I can work on direction.*
>
> – GABI NEUROHR

A. Follow my energy:

- Simple gait transitions (up and down)
- Trail rides in company of a calm horse
- Emergency stop (all three gaits)
- Maintain gait at the trot
- Back up from a trot
- Easy transitions to canter
- Canter on trail rides
- Canter around the arena
- Follow the arena rail pattern without too many corrections

B. Follow my focus:

- 20m circles (don't have to be perfectly round yet)
- Simple change of direction at the trot through the whole arena
- Half voltes and 10m voltes to work on direction (not required to be perfect yet either)
- Isolated yields of shoulders and hindquarter
- Point-to-point games (moving from A to B)
- Yielding sideways with the help of a wall
- Work with easy trail obstacles such as trotting poles
- Pole corridor
- Slalom
- Figure of eight
- Cross a wooden bridge
- Cross a plastic tarp

This stage will take between ten and thirty rides. It all depends on the horse's personality and disposition. Don't try to rush anything; take the time to do it well.

5. Accept the bit

Once the horse understands about following my energy and my focus, and I don't have to rely too much on the reins for control anymore, the horse is ready to accept the bit. The bit's primary function should always be to refine communication, not to control the horse or to force him to adopt a certain body position.

Some horses I ride without the bit, either because no matter what I tried, they just hated it or it's because

"You might wonder how to control a young horse without a bit. The key is to educate and form a strong connection to the horse—this will work better than any mechanical tool."

– Gabi Neurohr

I don't need to use a bit for the discipline I compete in. Why use a bit if I don't need to?

I introduce the bit rather late, for one reason: The mouth isn't only the most sensitive part of the horse's body, it is also the most sensitive place emotionally. When being started under saddle, the horse is confronted with many new impressions. Adding the bit early can amplify adverse reactions to it. If you want to make everything as easy and stress-free for your horse, introduce the bit later.

If ever you choose to ride with a bit and get your horse to accept the bit with confidence and without defensive reactions, help your horse master these three tasks:

- Accepting bridling, catching the bit
- Wearing the bridle
- Understanding and respecting the action of the bit: directional, downwards transitions, flexion

Completion of the colt start

A colt start is finished when you can:

- Ride your horse in all three gaits in the arena and out on trail rides;
- You can do simple turns and imperfect circles and navigate over simple trail obstacles; and
- You have a solid base of trust and understanding between your horse and yourself as the rider.

Usually completion takes between fifteen and thirty rides, depending on your skill level and the disposition of the horse. Now you are ready to continue your journey with giving your horse a solid foundation training.

Foundation training

The colt start gives the horse an introduction to his new job as a riding horse. It is very important that this first impression is good, but it also means that nothing is ingrained. The horse doesn't yet have the experience and the miles necessary to be a reliable, "functioning" partner.

I see this misconception so many times. Too many people expect the horse to be fully functional after he/she has been started or had thirty days of training; in fact, after the horse is started, he needs a solid foundation training. Unfortunately, I see too many horses enter specialization training right after they are started.

Through many hours in the saddle and repetitions, I refine the horse's understanding of the aids of my seat, legs, and reins. I teach the horse to work with healthy biomechanics, i.e., bending and working in a frame. I improve the horse's maneuverability through lateral movements.

During foundation training, the horse learns to understand more complex tasks, such as how to bend around the inside leg and how to execute half halts. The horse also learns to maintain his responsibilities of keeping gait and direction on circles and straight lines. This will help to develop a nice impulsion, meaning a horse who works in an even rhythm without rushing and without being lazy.

During the two years following the colt start, I expose the horse to as many different situations as possible, such as trail rides, trail courses, grid and jumping work, dressage work, cow work, riding in the neighbor stable, and minor competitions. I teach the horse to be brave and to trust me in different situations. What a horse can do at home doesn't necessarily apply in a different environment. The horse learns to become your partner through life experience. My aim is to create a solid and well-rounded foundation that serves me no matter what discipline I choose later. I want us to become partners.

Entry-level competitions

Young horse entry-level competitions come under the banner of foundation training. Specialization starts at medium-level competitions. Ideally, a dressage horse should able to jump around an entry-level jumping course, an endurance horse should be able to do an entry-level dressage test.

Maybe you have no ambition to compete long term, and that's fine. However, I think it is important to give your horse as many impressions as possible. Expose him, give him life experience, give him the hours under saddle he needs to become the solid and versatile partner you always dreamed of. A little competition outing here and there, just to get the experience, is absolutely worth the effort. Or just drive to your neighbor stable and join a group trail ride there.

Age-based roadmap

Let's imagine the perfect road of development for a horse: You either have a foal from your own mare or you bought a weanling, and you have the opportunity to lay a healthy foundation from very young age. The following is an outline for this ideal scenario for age-based learning.

Up to 1 year: Basic handling and utility skills

Primary goal: Build a positive association towards humans and learn the basic rules of living with together.

All the daily handling tasks you can teach a foal from day one. In chronological order, it would look like this:

- Accept touch and scratches
- Catching
- Grooming
- Haltering
- Picking up the feet

- Leading
- Accepting worm paste
- Respect at feeding time
- Yielding to pressure on a basic level
- Confrontation with unknown/strange objects
- Going for walks with its mother

The order will change with every foal, depending on character and disposition. At one year of age, a youngster should be easy to handle during the basic daily life challenges. He is easy to catch and halter, leads well within his known perimeters, confident when having his feet trimmed, respectful at feeding time, knows how to behave around people, confident but not pushy or naughty, moves when asked to move out of the way, and doesn't push through pressure.

Some foals are more confident than others and will already come willingly on walks with you alone—this is a plus but not a must at this age. They are only babies and still depend a lot on the company of other horses. Make sure he grows up with company of other horses, outside where he can run and play. Stall confinement and isolation are absolutely detrimental at this age.

Don't force anything at this age. Give your baby time to mature, to grow and to slowly become more confident and skilled.

Age 1-2 years: Advancing basic handling and utility skills

Primary goal: Build positive association with leaving the herd and spending time with a human.

Yearlings are very much like pre-adolescent children. They are playful and eager to explore, and they still have childlike innocence. They are starting to become more independent but still like to run back to friends or parent/guardian when they feel insecure.

This is the perfect age to start taking him on walks alone and to develop a certain level of independence. Go and explore the world together with him. Show him as many things as possible. Take a second horse with you at first to make sure not to push him over an emotional cliff into the red zone (more about this in Chapter 12). He should grow in confidence and complete every walk with a good feeling.

In your learning program for your yearling, advance the basic skills and learn new utility skills.

With advancing the basic skills, for example, your yearling will learn to trot in hand and synchronize with you. He will learn to hold his hooves up longer to have them trimmed. He starts to stand still for grooming without being tied.

Now is also a good time to start some light groundwork with your yearling, where he should learn the basic yields and some confidence-building exercises.

Focus on getting everything a little better by repetition and reward him at the right time.

He should learn the utility skills. Be patient when teaching them, go slowly and casually.

Your youngster should learn to:

- Accept the shower
- Be confident with the clipper and fly spray
- Accept being tied up
- Stand still without being tied for grooming
- Accept trailer loading
- Farrier preparations
- Accept vet handling (needles, taking temperature, applying bandages, checking eyes)

All these skills are taught best at this age, but don't worry about getting them 100 percent perfect yet. All you want is that your horse tries, understands, and is confident. Accept it when he tells you that it's too much. Don't hesitate to take a second horse with you that can give the young horse a bit of extra confidence, especially for tasks like trailer loading, tying, showering, or going on longer walks. Think of every possible way to make learning easy and even fun for your youngster.

Always keep the primary goal in mind and don't get lost in the tasks.

Age 2-3 years: Foundational groundwork

Primary goal: Build a positive association towards learning and arenas.

Many youngsters will have a bit of a rebellious phase at this age. They discover their strength and often they discover that they can dominate a younger or weaker herd member. Their confidence grows, so they naturally want to see what they can do.

You can compare a two-year-old horse with an adolescent child. This is the age they discover opinions of their own and become more and more independent and self-confident. But the world still collapses from time to time, and they need the safety and loving reassurance of family. Be ready to go through this stage with confidence. Don't get desperate or frustrated—it will pass.

During this year, you can prepare your horse for his start under saddle. Do plenty of groundwork to boost his confidence, and build communication so that he willingly allows you to control his gaits and direction of travel. You can also teach him to pony if you have a reliable older riding horse. You can already get him used to the cinch and the saddle. If you are skilled, you can teach him to long line, which is a great preparation for riding later.

From two and a half years, you can also slowly start to prepare your horse to be physically fit for the next step. You can help him to be well coordinated and to activate and strengthen the right muscles to carry a rider later. Cavalletti work, jogging, off-road trail walks, and in-hand dressage work on the caveson are fantastic ways to prepare your horse physically.

Take your time and don't do too much: your horse is still growing! Don't overwork your horse into a sweat, especially not when working on a circle! Some horses are physically mature enough to slowly start doing a little work, whereas others are simply late developers. Keep in mind that skeletal maturity isn't complete until five and a half to six years old. Some growth plates even only fuse at seven years old. This doesn't mean that you need to wait to do any work until your horse is six, but there is no problem if you wait until three years old or even as late as five years old before introducing normal work. Listen to your horse and make sure you have everything right from a nutritional point of view when introducing work. Before the normal work begins, let him socialize and be a horse.

Age 3-4 years: The colt start

Primary goal: Build a positive association towards being ridden.

This is the most exciting year—it's time to start your horse under saddle. Whether you do it yourself or send your horse to a trusted trainer, this is a big step. Keep in mind, however, that a horse isn't fully grown until five to seven years; therefore, you really just want to start him, not work him.

It works well to advance in two-month blocks of work: two months on, two months off. With some horses, I just do ten rides and then turn the horse back out for six months to finish growing. If everything is well done and the horse was fully engaged in the process, he won't forget a thing. Each time I ride them again, even if it is a whole year later, everything is right where I left off.

Before starting your youngster, you want to be sure that your horse is physically and mentally ready for this new challenge. Here is a checklist before you start your horse under saddle:

1. **Dental check.** Schedule a visit of a qualified equine dentist if you intend to ride your horse with a bit (making sure he has no wolf's teeth).
2. **Osteopathic check.** Have your horse checked by an osteopath to make sure he has no blockages in is body causing him to be uncomfortable. The osteopath will also help you to assess if your horse is strong enough and ready to carry a rider. Some youngsters have all the wrong muscles and first need to develop better biomechanics and learn how to use their body in a way that they can support and balance the weight of a rider.
3. **Hoof check.** Make sure that the hooves are in great shape in advance and that your horse is comfortable on his feet.
4. **Weight assessment.** Make sure your horse is not too skinny. Going into work means a lot to young horses. They are still growing and will need quite a bit more food to compensate for the extra physical effort.

Once you have checked all this, you are ready to go!

The process of starting a horse is an important time, perhaps the most important time in your horse's life—so many new impressions, new challenges, new sensations, new inputs. Make sure to offer your horse a lot of consistency during this time. For the best learning results and best progress, work your horse three to six times per week. The sessions don't have to be long or intense, but they should be regular and well structured. Offer your horse the comfort and reassurance of a predictable rhythm.

If you give your horse to a trainer, s/he will take care of that. If you decide to do this step yourself, choose a period when you are able to spend a lot of time with your horse; for example, your summer holiday.

I can't stress this enough: the colt start is the most important event in your youngster's life! Choose the timing of it wisely. You want to be able to do at least ten rides in a short period of time. Do it well, invest time, and invest in qualified support.

As you progress step by step, you will slowly migrate to the next stage of development.

Age 4-6 Years: Foundation training

Primary goal: Create a well-rounded and versatile horse that loves his job and is a pleasure to ride.

Now it's time to "put on the miles," as a lot of people like to say. It takes approximately two years of regular work for a horse to really know his job.

During these two years, you teach your horse good solid basics. There will be a lot of routine and repetition. It's easy to fall into the trap to just ride along and not have a real plan. You should still follow a plan, have an objective, and always keep the bigger picture in mind. Progress is slower in this stage, or so it seems. It is easy to lose track or get frustrated because you don't see the progress as much as you did in previous stages.

During foundation training, it is about raising the quality of existing skills.

What helps a lot is to keep to one subject for three months and then proceed to the next one. On this schedule, one year would look like this:

1. **Month 1–3:** Teach the horse to move with rhythm and relaxation in all three gaits and do all the arena figures. Focus on relaxation while maintaining responsiveness. To keep work from becoming too intense, play with the horse on the ground or at liberty every second or third session.
2. **Month 4–6:** Focus on trail rides. To maintain and still advance the work of the previous three months, change between arena work and trail rides.
3. **Month 7–9:** Focus on grid work. Do cavalletti work and walk, trot, and maybe canter while maintaining the qualities you worked on during the first three months. I would throw in a trail ride every week and a groundwork session every week.
4. **Month 9–12:** Go and ride at a neighbor's stable once a week if possible. Split the rest of the weekly sessions between the other topics focused on previously.

During foundation training, you still want to keep work regular, but you don't need to work your horse as consistently and often as during his start under saddle. Three sessions per week are enough to make plenty of progress. Of course, if you manage to dedicate more time, all the better! Just keep in mind your horse is still growing and needs days to recover after more strenuous exercise days. Keep a plan that balances variety with consistency.

During the second year, you want to go deeper into each subject and expose your horse to more new environments, maybe go on a few first competitions for fun if you are interested in that. Or go for a weeklong trail ride with some friends. Keep work casual while constantly seeking to improve your horse's understanding of the aids, biomechanics, and emotional, mental and physical fitness.

If you choose to specialize your horse in a discipline after this training, you'll start off with a horse that has a broad set of basic skills, and they will progress quickly in the discipline of choice.

Alternatively, simply choose to specialize your horse in being your friend and leisure partner, have some fun play at liberty, go on long trail rides, or have a lot of fun on the ground. Especially for our leisure partners it is important to have a solid foundation training. Help your horse to understand all the activities that you want to undertake together.

Remember, following a clear roadmap makes sure that your horse has a solid foundation for life. A blueprint ensures that your horse is always ready for the next step. Your horse will understand the next step easily, he will feel successful, content and confident, and he will become a happy learner.

Only when the steps are too big or the previous step was skipped, will the horse react defensively due to lack of understanding. In short, most of the drama, emotional outbreaks, and defensive behavior can be largely prevented by following a clear roadmap step by step.

Exercise: Create your roadmap

In Chapter 9 of the workbook, you'll discover a template that helps you draft a year-long educational plan for your horse.

If you haven't downloaded the workbook yet, you can get it here: https://www.understandingisthekey.com/workbook

Take the time to build this solid foundation from the ground up, step by step, and you will save yourself and your horse lots of trouble and time later. You will be able to enjoy your horse more if you dedicate this time in your horse's early years.

Create a Solid Training Plan

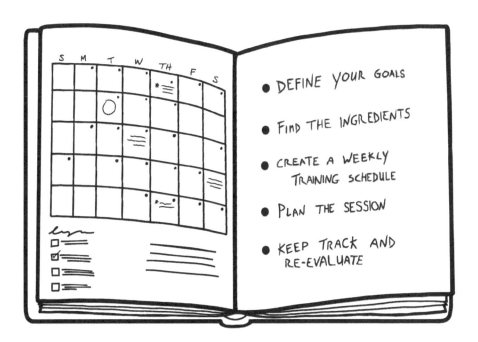

- DEFINE YOUR GOALS
- FIND THE INGREDIENTS
- CREATE A WEEKLY TRAINING SCHEDULE
- PLAN THE SESSION
- KEEP TRACK AND RE-EVALUATE

U ntil now you have learned so much about how horses learn, how they think, and how they perceive the world. You have explored your own motivations and what drives you and discovered a little bit more about what it takes to become a responsible horse owner. Now it is time to get practical and learn how to apply all that you now know to everyday life with your horse.

How do you climb Mount Everest? Step by step. Sometimes the size of the mountain in front of us makes us lose hope and freeze in fear of failure. Or we just go for it, full of enthusiasm but without a real plan and run out of energy as soon as the first hurdles appear in our way.

To avoid becoming overwhelmed by all the information and everything you must take into consideration, it is crucial to have a plan. Having structure and keeping track of progress and problems set you up for success. By planning, you make sure to stay on track, consistently making little steps towards your goal. It gives you and your horse a structure to hold on to, even if your instructor/coach is far away or you don't have the money to afford regular lessons.

By making a plan, your goals actually become attainable one step at a time. If you don't plan, your goals stay dreams and you will run behind them forever.

Goals have to be SMART

This is a widely used management concept I learned many years ago that helped me be very clear in my goals.

Your goals should be

- Specific
- Measurable

- Attainable
- Relevant
- Time-bound

Specific

You can say something like, "I want to improve the relationship." But how do you want your relationship with your horse to look and feel? How will your horse behave towards you? Be specific in the description of your goal, and be clear about what exactly you want to achieve. Also be specific with tasks. How many steps sideways, how many laps of canter, how many miles per trail ride? Nail it all down.

You can ask yourself these questions: What do I want to achieve? Where? How?

Measurable

Set targets for what you will see, hear, feel and do in the pursuit of your goal. Feeling connected to your horse is not measurable. What will the connection look like? What will your horse do and how will he respond to you? You might want to improve your confidence on trail rides, but this is not measurable. Rather, say, "I will go on two thirty-minute trail rides with a good friend each week. I will feel at ease."

Attainable

Attainable means that your goals are realistic for you and your horse's abilities. This means that you don't try to teach your quarter horse to go for a 1.10m (4ft) show jumping competition. Now, maybe the five-year goal seems to be unattainable right now, but it will come in reach with all the three-month goals achieved. Also, is your goal attainable with your financial resources? With the time you can put into it? With your current level of skill?

Relevant

Is a particular goal that you set really relevant to the main goal you want to achieve? Does it lead you in the direction you want to go or does it actually sidetrack you? Ask yourself why you want to reach this specific goal. What is the objective behind the goal and will the goal really help you achieve this objective?

Time-bound

Set a deadline for achieving the goal. This will help you to switch from just making plans to action. I work really well when I have time pressure. I know it is not the smartest way to function, but setting myself a date for achieving a certain task helps me to get up and going. Now, of course, your horse is in charge of the timeline, so you have to keep the timeline realistic to your horse, your speed of learning, the time you can sacrifice every week to spend with your horse. If you get too pushy with yourself and the timelines, you will get too pushy with your horse. Set a timeline, but be gentle and flexible about it. What you can do though is, to commit to a weekly time you will spend with your horse.

Find your starting point

Before you head off to define your goals, you need to find your starting point. This is where you have to be brutally honest with yourself about where you're at and what resources you have. But don't paint too dark a picture and hold yourself down either! Be realistic.

Evaluate where you are at with your horse right now in these areas:

1. Relationship
2. Basic handling
3. Groundwork
4. Riding
5. Personal goals

Relationship

This is about facts, not emotions. If you find yourself making claims like, "I feel that my horse doesn't like to spend time with me," emotions may be involved. But emotions are always subjective and vary from day to day. It's okay and normal to have them, but in this exercise, leave them out. You need the facts about your situation so that you have a starting point and can measure your progress from there.

Basic handling

This is about the everyday tasks. How well does your horse lead? How well does he allow you to handle his feet? What about trailer loading, respect at feeding time, or standing still for grooming? How well is your horse socialized with horses and humans? Check the previous chapter for the complete list.

Groundwork

How well does your horse understand you when working on the ground? How well does your horse yield in all directions to both steady and rhythmic pressure? How willing is your horse to give you control over gait and direction? How confident is your horse around all kind of different stimuli, like tarp, umbrellas, stick and string, plastic flag and so on?

Riding

Where are you at with your riding? What's working and what's not working so well? Keep in mind to always evaluate the facts: *no emotions.* Use a rating system to objectively assess every aspect of your horse's skills under saddle. You want to rate how well your horse executes upward and downward transitions, how he allows you to direct him, how well he responds to your leg aids, etc. How confident is he out on trails and at home? Look at how he uses his body: Is he flexible and strong or does he feel out of balance and stiff?

Personal goals

What are your personal goals? We need a lot of knowledge if we want to take care for a horse properly. Hoof care, nutrition, saddle fitting, emergency care, tool handling, riding skills, etc. The list is long. How much do you know? Be honest with yourself so that you can make the right decisions to learn what is most important for you and your horse. Maybe you want to learn about equine health and nutrition so that you can make smart decisions and aren't so dependent on what is written on the label of the food bag and other professionals' opinions anymore. Or you want to improve your physical fitness and riding skills by starting a Pilates class and taking riding lessons in order to be fit for your young horse once he is old enough to ride. Setting objectives for personal learning is just as important as it is to set goals for your horse's learning.

If you have a hard time to evaluate things objectively, ask a friend to watch you or video a session with your horse to get a picture.

Now you have your first list: the facts in each category of where you are right now.

Define your goals

Now it's time to define your goals in three more lists. Ask yourself:

- What is my long-term or biggest goal?
- What is my medium, or one-year, goal?
- What is my short-term goal or three-month goal?

First, define your long-term goals in all five categories mentioned above. Write them down. The simple act of writing things down lets them come alive. Writing them down is the very first step to acting on reaching your goals.

Now you know what you want to achieve with your horse in several years. Remember to not make the goal too small. Of course, being the horseperson you are right now might mean you're not able to achieve that, but you are going to grow. The horseperson you are going to be in several years has nothing to do with who you are now. So, even if you can't imagine being at that point now, don't set your goal too small.

Your next step is to define where you want to be in one year. And then, define the short-term goals you want to achieve within the next three months.

So, now you should have four big lists:

- List 1 with all the facts in each category where you are right now
- List 2 with your long-term goals
- List 3 with your goals for in one year
- List 4 with your goals for the next three months

Find the ingredients

Now you need to find the ingredients for your goals. Let's start with your three-month goals; those which are the closest and you have to tackle next.

When teaching a horse a task, you always want to think about how you can isolate, separate and recombine.

Take trailer loading for example. There are many little preparations you can do away from the trailer to prepare your horse to be confident with stepping on a different surface, handling the noise it makes, standing still, being tied and being in a tight space. If you practice all the ingredients with success, chances are your horse will load pretty easily into the trailer when you recombine all the elements you practiced separately.

Think about all the ingredients you need to achieve a certain task. If you just practice the task, chances are high that you will confuse your horse. Learn to break everything down into small, digestible steps. Once all the steps work and your horse can easily do them, put it all together. You will see that even complicated tasks suddenly become easy.

Once you know the ingredients, you need to achieve a certain task successfully, go and create your weekly session schedule. Fit the pieces of the puzzle together. This is one of the main secrets of spending a happy time with your horse: the ability to chop every complex task down into many little steps. If you do this consistently, learning will be easy for your horse and you will both start to feel successful and happy after each session.

Create your schedule

Either create a weekly structure or a structure for the next four to seven sessions if you can't spend a lot of time with your horse every week. The reason that four to seven sessions works is that the horse needs consistency and repetition. Return to Chapter 6 on Equine Learning if you need to review.

Pick a task from each category from your three-month goal list. Pick the one that seems the most urgent and find the ingredients you need to succeed in this task. Then put the ingredients in your session plan. Here's an example of three-month goals for my two-year-old filly.

1. Relationship: comes with me away from the herd without stopping and calling
2. Basic handling: accepts shower, stands patiently for hoof care
3. Groundwork: yields to pressure softly in all directions, accept cinch, goes on walks alone
4. Riding: not yet
5. Personal goals: learn about equine biomechanics

Here is the list of ingredients it takes to achieve those goals:

1. Relationship: Visit her as often as possible to spend time with her and give her scratches, take her to go grazing just outside of the field, teach her to be clear about respecting my space.

2. Basic handling: Teach her to stand still in the grooming corner (while grooming) without being tied, massage her legs, teach her to pick up her feet by a light touch on the chestnut, get her confident with the area of the shower, the noise and sensation of water.
3. Groundwork: Take her out of the field alone but stay in a known environment, teach her to back up, lower the head, disengage hindquarters, accept a surcingle later the bareback pad.
4. Riding: None yet.
5. Personal goals: look up a good book about equine biomechanics.

Plan according to the horse's personality

Within your weekly structure, you want to consider your horse's personality. Is s/he a horse that is very active and confident or more a fearful, unsure type? A confident horse will need more variety in the weekly schedule. An unconfident type will need more consistency and repetition.

When you offer more variety, you still want to follow a blueprint, a principal goal: don't go all over the place with the subjects. Let's take the example of eighteen-month-old horse who's a very confident and fast learner. Let's say I have seven sessions.

Day 1: Visit in the field, spend ten minutes, halter, practice backing up, then go grazing outside the field and explore some interesting things close by.
Day 2: Visit in the field, spend ten minutes, halter, practice backing up + head down briefly, go to the grooming area, groom while practicing standing still.
Day 3: Visit in the field, spend ten minutes, halter, backing up + head down + disengage hindquarters, go for a little tour outside the field to explore everything (stay in sight of the other horses).
Day 4: Visit in the field, spend ten minutes, take some time to practice putting the head in the halter, back up + head down +

disengage hindquarters, go to the grooming area, groom while standing still, massage legs and teach to lift them when touching the chestnut.

Day 5: Visit in the field, haltering, rub all over with the lead rope, lower the head, back up, disengage hindquarters both ways, go for a little trip outside the field (this time a little bit further), end in the grooming corner where we practice standing still while grooming, massage legs and pick them up by a light touch of the chestnut. When I bring him back to the field, spend ten minutes grazing in front of the gate.

Use day six and day seven to confirm and refine.

With an unconfident type of horse, you need to keep every session almost exactly the same until the horse is confident with this activity. Then you can teach your horse another activity, until he is confident doing that. And so on. When you have three activities your horse is confident with, then you can start to alternate between them.

This principle stays the same, no matter how educated your horse is. Confident horses need more variety in the weekly schedule to stay interested and mentally engaged. Unconfident horses need consistency to feel safe and to be able to anticipate.

Plan the session

Now that you have your weekly schedule, you want to also make a plan or general structure for your next session.

Each session has three parts: the warm-up, the working phase or teaching phase, and the cool down.

Warm-up

This happens during the first five to twenty minutes of your session, depending on your horse's need and what you plan to do. It's not only about the physical warm-up, but mainly about the mental and emotional warm-up. The goal is to bring your horse into the "learning frame of mind."

What do you have to do to get your horse to be connected to you, confident with his environment, and motivated to learn new things? Maybe you need to start with an exercise your horse knows very well and likes to do. Or you have to focus on calming your horse if he is very excited. You want to get your horse to a point where he wants to put effort for you.

This will be different with every horse, depending on personality and stage of education. And what your horse needs to be in a good learning frame of mind can change from day to day.

Working/teaching

Once your horse is connected, calm, and motivated to work, you can now teach your horse a new task or work on improving an exercise. I usually have two to three tasks/patterns in this phase. One of the tasks/patterns the horse has done already about four times and knows how to do it but must practice the skill. One of the tasks the horse has done about two times before and has started to understand but still lacks refinement. And, finally, one new task. The tasks can be related, which helps for the horse's general understanding. You want to keep this phase as short as possible. Short and to the point—look for little improvements, not perfection. Make your horse feel proud about his achievements and let him know how smart he is.

Cool down

This phase is to cool down the body and return to a calm mind. Sometimes learning can be exciting, so this is the time to return to a state of calm and relaxation. You want to do something easy to finish the session. With a more educated horse, I will practice some precise yields, just to finish the session on something quiet and to cool down the body. With a young horse, I might allow him to roll or do some of his favorite exercises. You can take your horse grazing or go for a short walk your horse knows.

Horses will mainly remember the last emotion they had before you put them back in their field. This is why this phase is very important. You want your horse to leave the session with a positive feeling.

Here's an example for a one- or two-year-old:

- Warm up: Spend ten minutes with the horse in the field, scratches, haltering.
- Working: Standing still in the grooming area, go for a little walk and touch any strange object.
- Cool down: Go back to the field, graze for ten minutes before returning your horse to to his friends in the field.

Here's an example for a five- or six-year-old:
- Warm up: Walk around the arena, transitions, halt; walk, watch out for spooky spots and deal with them; practice random leg yields in a playful way.
- Working: Refine trot-canter transitions, serpentines at the trot, double transitions.
- Cool down: Walk on a long rein, practice steering with just the legs, ten-minute walk around the property, allow a good roll.

Keep track, rate and reevaluate

Keep track of every session and reevaluate your position after four to seven sessions. I have a rating system ranging from 0–10 for every exercise I currently work on.

Let's say my two-year-old needs to learn to patiently give his feet to have them trimmed. A rating of 10 would be given if he is standing still perfectly, giving all four feet and not trying to pull them away. At a 3 rating, he is not standing still on his own, or will only stand for a maximum of thirty seconds before I have to correct him. He willingly gives his feet, but pulls them away after about thirty seconds, barely long enough time to pick them out.

After five to seven sessions working on this, I reevaluate. How long can he stand still now before I have to correct him? How long does he give me his feet now? What rating can I give it now?

Now you can see why it is so important to write down the facts about every exercise: How long, how many steps, how many laps, and so on, until you have to correct your horse. This is your reference guide, and it will make it very clear to you whether you are progressing or not.

Often it will feel as if you aren't progressing at all, but most often once you look at the facts from one month ago, you will see that actually you progressed pretty nicely.

We tend to think that progress is only when things are working perfectly. That is a rotten tooth that needs to be pulled! Thinking in this way leaves us frustrated and stagnant, and our horse is frustrated too because we are never happy.

Perfection is a lie. Look at the progress you make and be happy about it.

What if your rating/quality went down? That is not a big deal. The worst you can do is to beat yourself up over it. Realize your mistake and make a new plan using different learning strategies to course-correct. Learning is also about what doesn't work; this is just as important. No guilt, no shame—only new decisions.

Don't let failures take you down, discourage you, or stop you from going to your horse. I know from my own experience that these moments can feel pretty dark. But do you know the good news about these moments? They activate your brain to find a new solution, to think in new ways. Problems mean progress.

If things get too tough, you have two choices: drop the difficult topic and just don't look at it for a good while or ask for support to help you untangle the knot.

Exercise:
Make your action plan

If you haven't downloaded the workbook yet, you can get it here: https://www.understandingisthekey.com/workbook

Once you have it, turn to chapter 10 to define your long-term goals. There, you'll also discover a handy template to help you plan your next seven sessions with your horse.

Progress is never linear; it comes with many ups and downs. Creating a solid plan, keeping track and consistently reevaluating will help you to progress faster. You'll also realize sooner when things don't go in the right direction so that you can course-correct and adjust. It takes discipline to keep track, to follow a plan and to not just go and do whatever with your horse. Nobody can help you to find the motivation to push through and to actually start taking action towards your dream; only you can do that. So, go and make your plan of action!

Create Your Dream Relationship

The process of shaping and educating a young horse and trying to create a dream horse is long and complex. Some people think about all the tasks and things the horse has to learn to master everyday life and to become a reliable riding horse, but there is one important aspect that holds everything together like glue: the relationship you have with your horse.

There is no doubt about the power of a positive relationship with your horse: it's magic, it's wonderful, and it's hard to describe or to explain to any non-horse person. Even now, as I write this, it is difficult for me to put into words. I just know that if I have a strong relationship based on mutual respect and love with my horse, together we can reach new heights; together we can be stronger, we can dance, we can read each other's thoughts. We will overcome dark spots and difficulties more easily together.

> *"There is no secret so close as that held between a girl and her horse."*
>
> - UNKNOWN

Unfortunately, this relationship doesn't happen overnight. It's not right there as soon as your new horse moves in. You have to CREATE it. You have to nurture it so that it can grow over time. You can do this consciously, rather than leaving it up to chance.

Cultivate awareness

How do you want the relationship between the two of you to feel and look like? How would you like your horse to feel and behave towards you? What do you wish for yourself? How do you want the two of you to interact with each other?

I don't know what kind of relationship you want to have. Everybody is different in that way. Some people just want to play at liberty and dream about their horse coming at full gallop to the gate. They might not mind so much if the horse sometimes doesn't follow their ideas.

Other people might put more importance on their horse being respectful at all times and reliable in everyday life and when riding. Having their horse greet them at the gate might not be so important to them.

And then there is the third option, where the horse still comes to meet you at the gate *and* is a respectful and reliable partner. One doesn't necessarily exclude the other. This is my high standard I like to reach. You must make up your mind which one you would like. Draw yourself a mental picture of how you would like the friendship with your horse to be.

Of course, this also depends a lot on the individual horse. But you are the leader; you form and create the relationship because horses naturally imitate emotion and attitudes. So, how do you want this relationship to feel? You have to carry this mental picture and feel with you at all times.

Remember you are as important as your horse

For a friendship to work, both individuals need to feel important. Sometimes we horse owners, especially women, put our horse on a pedestal and try to make everything right for the horse. We might say, "He didn't mean it like that" or "He spooked, that's why he jumped on my toe," or "He got distracted, so he couldn't listen." We tend to make our horses so much more important than us.

What about giving yourself and what you want some importance as well?

Be real to your horse and don't cover up your wishes and limits just to please your horse or to avoid upsetting him. If you let your horse walk all over you, he will do it simply because he can. It is you who must make this impossible to him and make it very clear that you would like to be respected as a person, just as much as you respect your horse.

Be natural, be you, don't fake anything because then you will not be able to hold up your standards for very long. Be authentic and don't ever lose sight of the end goal. Your horse is also just himself towards you, expressing every thought and sentiment unfiltered. Do the same and be natural, be you.

Four stages of the relationship

The harmonious dream relationship doesn't happen right away. It's a process and it usually happens in four stages, and it's only the last and final stage that feels as if my horse can read my mind and harmony has been established.

Get to know each other

The very first stage is to learn to know each other. You can't expect your horse to trust or respect you right away without knowing you. Give your horse time to get familiar with your smell, the sound of your voice, your appearance and your way of acting. Get to know your horse. What is he/she worried about? What does he/she like/dislike? What is his/her personality?

Establish clear boundaries

This is the stage where a many people say, "The horse is testing his boundaries." Often in this stage there will be conflicts. Who is the one who takes the decisions in the relationship when things get tough? It should be you, so in this stage, it is important to set clear boundaries. Make sure to be very clear about your limits and about who moves whom. No need to get emotional or angry about it; just be aware and make sure you don't hesitate to insist on your limits and on what you want.

It always takes some time until everybody finds his/her place in a relationship. Give yourself and your horse this time to feel comfortable with each other's limits, likes and dislikes.

Don't fear the clearing thunderstorm—face it! Otherwise you might stay stuck in this rather uncomfortable stage for a long time. The sooner you can find the guts to face the storm, the sooner it is over. The more reliable you are in upholding these boundaries, the sooner your horse will trust and respect you.

Routines

After the eventual storm has cleared and everybody has found his/her place in the relationship, quiet routines can take over. Clear structures are established and the two of you start to feel comfortable together. You become a team and work towards a goal. You are both learning the skills necessary.

During this stage, you train and educate your horse. You train and educate yourself. You grow together. You know each other better and better. Your horse knows the routine of when you come to do something together. Mostly, your time together is free of stress and excitement, unless you do something new and out of the routine.

Harmony

You spent so much time and effort educating your horse and yourself, now you know each other inside out. Now you start to feel truly in harmony. You have moments where you have the impression as if your horse can read your thoughts. You trust your horse, and your horse trusts you. You become a unit and know each other inside out. Now the full potential of the two of you gets revealed. Disagreements or discussions and moments of fear become very rare. You are in sync and complement each other.

Everybody wants to be in the last stage as soon as possible, if not right away. So many of my clients feel disappointed and take it personally when their horse doesn't come running or when their horse tests his limits and doesn't listen. This is just a stage in the growing relationship! I get it: I too wish it were always simply harmonious.

Build a relationship based on love and boundaries

Now that you know how you want your friendship to be and to feel to you, how can you let this mental picture come alive? Your horse has no idea about your plans. In fact, horses are perfectly happy without us humans. If they live in a herd, have food and water, can move and play, they really don't need us. So, how can you convince your horse to want to spend time with you without forcing it? How can you make your idea about the relationship become your horse's idea?

There are two main elements: love and boundaries. They're all linked. You can't have respect without fear if your horse isn't confident, and you can't have real confidence if you have no reliable boundaries.

There are the "Love People" and the "Respect People." The horses of the Love People are very human-friendly but might be quite pushy at times and not listen when it counts. The horses of the Respect People mostly listen well and have perfect manners but often execute their duty with a poor attitude. You need to find the balance between the two. It can be a real juggling act at times.

Let's first talk about the love or confidence aspect. Your horse needs to trust you, fully. Your horse needs to have a positive association towards you. How can you build this?

If you think of another person, you will have either a positive or a negative sense of them. This association, once formed, stays pretty much the same for a long time. Quite something has to happen for it to change. Our interactions with that person will be colored by that positive or negative association, if we want it or not.

Same with our horses. Does your horse have positive emotions towards you, or more negative ones? The way your horse behaves towards you depends heavily on the association he/she has developed. He will be either reserved and shy or open and interested.

In scientific terms this would be called Classical Conditioning. You condition your horse to see and perceive you as something positive in his life.

Spend undemanding time

Visit your horse and spend undemanding time. Ask nothing of your horse, nothing—not even that your horse stays close to you or comes to say hello. Just be with your horse, watch his routines and find out who his friends are. When he wants to be close to you, find his/her itchy spots. Give him plenty of scratches and be your horses grooming buddy. Or you can take your horse and just go grazing. It's all about spending a nice time with your horse. Do the things with your horse he will love. Soon he/she will start looking forward to your visits. This is how you can very easily add many points to your relationship scorecard.

Be the provider, the caretaker

Another very powerful way to create a positive association towards you is to be your horse's provider. If possible, be the one who feeds your horse, who brings the water. Be the one who takes care of your horse's comfort and well-being. Especially when feeding your horse, you can immensely improve your relationship. Not only do you provide something pleasant, this is also an excellent opportunity to establish respect. Horses naturally clear their hierarchy over food and water.

Be the protector

Protect your horse from other, more dominant horses when you are with him in the field. Especially if your horse is low ranking, you can collect a lot of friend points that way. Soon your horse will see you as his safe haven and leader when you are with him. Protect your herd of two, like a mare protects her foal so that your horse can feel safe around other horses when you are there. You can do something similar when going for a walk or on a trail ride. When your horse is afraid, go and walk between the source of fear and your horse. You act as the barrier, the protector. Your horse feels seen and respected in his fear, instead of pushed and exposed.

Love like a parent

We need to put our heart in our hands and touch our horses with our heart. Yes, but to love our horse doesn't only mean always being nice. If you have kids, you know that very well. We need to set boundaries, give our horses limits. This will help them to know where they are at and help them to feel safe.

How to set healthy boundaries

The majority of horse owners I meet are very good in loving their horses. But they aren't so good when it comes to setting boundaries.

Remember the story of the four-year-old Welsh pony called Erowan? He was the cutest pony ever with his big eyes, a pretty face, and little pointy ears. The owners brought him to me because he was misbehaving quite a bit. In fact, he had become quite dangerous for their four-year-old daughter. The father told me a story about how Erowan usually behaved when they took him out on a walk. Their little daughter was riding Erowan, and the father would lead the pony to ensure the daughter's safety. But whenever Erowan would detect some nice green grass on the side of the path, he would go for it. The father said: "The only thing I could do was to quickly grab my daughter to ensure her safety." They didn't dare set clear limits for the pony because they were worried that they would hurt him. The father was a tall strong guy; the pony was little guy of only 1.10m. It would have been so easy for the father to hold and block the pony. This is just one of the many stories they told me about their "unruly" pony.

They were incapable of setting any limits, and the pony knew it. He did whatever he wanted to do, like a wild and playful teenage boy.

Let me ask you a simple question. What is more important: the safety of the girl or the short-term comfort of the horse?

To set boundaries and to insist on them during every single interaction is just as important for building a happy and healthy relationship as it is to love our horse. In fact, it goes hand in hand. But how can we do this in a way that our horse doesn't get afraid of us and that we can feel good about? Because, let's face it, you probably hate it as much as me when you must be firm with your horse.

This topic was quite a big struggle for me for a long time. I didn't want to hurt my horse, and I didn't want to lose trust. I found myself in a weird spiral: my horse wouldn't listen to me, she would push on me and plain ignore me. I would try to stay calm and patient for some time until it was just too much, and when I finally set the limit, I did it way too strongly. And this meant I had exactly what I wanted to avoid: my horse became afraid of me, and I felt terrible.

One day, I could observe an older experienced mare with some foals she was the nanny for. All the foals just magically seemed to respect her but without being afraid of her. Where the foals sometimes playfully nipped or kicked others, they never even attempted it with her. She had this incredible presence and didn't need to assert herself in a physical way. Calm, sovereign, sure of herself, she knew exactly how she would like the foals to behave around her.

She was the safe haven, the point of reference for all the foals. Everybody loved and trusted her.

How did she do that?

How the mother insists on boundaries

When my own mare Mazirah had a foal, she was quite tolerant with little Maserati the first few weeks. She didn't even say much when he accidentally kicked her or ran into her.

As Maserati got older, though, Mazirah started to be stricter with him, especially when nursing. He had to be polite and careful, otherwise she would bite his butt. When he was behaving very rudely, she would even kick him. She wouldn't let him have a drink until he stood nicely and calmly and asked politely for permission. Like this, he learned to accept a "no" and to say "please" and "thank you."

Mazirah never acted aggressively or mean with him, but she got her point across effectively and with the required firmness. She never lost her temper when she had to repeat herself over and over. The way she corrected him was also worth taking note of: before she got physical, she always gave a vocal warning.

By observing Mazirah, I discovered four things:

1. We should know what we want with a quiet and self-assured presence.
2. Have a firm and friendly attitude when we have to assert rules.
3. Warn verbally before correcting physically.
4. Get the point across 100 percent.

How do we manage these challenges? Where do quiet self-assurance and the ability to be firm and friendly at the same time come from?

Get clear about your rules

First of all, you need to get clear about the social rules you would like your youngster to maintain when with you. Don't let anyone tell you what your horse is allowed to do or not do. Free yourself of the opinion of other people and all the shoulds and shouldn'ts.

Ask yourself: What feels right to YOU? What behavior of your horse makes you feel irritated or unsafe? As soon as you feel irritated or just slightly unsafe, this is a boundary you should hold up. This is your little voice you should listen to as talked about in Chapter 3. Your feelings are just as important as your horse's. Soon the little disrespect will turn into a big problem, so learn to say and do something at the first sign to avoid big drama later. You are valuable and you have the right to stand up for yourself.

Keep in mind how you would like your horse to behave once he is an adult. If you allow him to bite your pockets for treats now, he will do it even more once he is older. If you allow your horse to push on you now, how will it be once he is fully grown? How much harder will it be to correct? Some things might be cute as long as the horse only weighs 100-200kg, but it might get unsafe once you imagine him 300kg heavier.

Make a list of all your rules. It could look a bit like this:

1. No biting
2. Don't push on me or crowd me
3. No ears-back attitude towards me or other people
4. I am no play buddy, so don't try to play foal games with me
5. No rearing when I am close
6. Don't pull on the halter
7. Don't run through pressure
8. Be polite when feeding

Making such a list will help you to get clarity about boundaries for yourself. This will give you better timing when you must set them.

Keep in mind that everybody is different with a different point of view, and that's why your list of rules might be different to someone else's. Just make sure it feels good to you. Only then you can stick with them consistently.

Remember, there is nothing worse than ever-changing rules and never knowing what to expect, even more so for a horse you want to trust and respect you as a leader. Real trust comes from being reliable and consistent, and always upholding the same boundaries.

How do you manage to be firm and friendly at the same time?

A common problem is to be either too soft to be effective or to act out of frustration/anger. This will cause the foal to get either cocky or afraid. Remembering these points will help you keep emotions out of the game:

1. He is a horse; he lives in the moment. Horses aren't plotting against their owners. No need to take things personally.
2. Boundaries give security and build the framework where the horse can feel safe. Imagine you aren't really sure what you are allowed to do. The sooner somebody tells you clearly, the sooner you can feel safe. So, just help your horse to feel safe sooner.
3. Horses only get afraid of you if you correct them while being emotional and when you keep emotions going on afterwards. And when you are emotional, your timing and intensity are rarely spot on.

But why do we so easily get emotional when we have to set boundaries for our horse? We get emotional when we aren't sure of ourselves anymore and when we think we might not do things perfectly or when we feel that we have to act against our inner values.

Give a verbal warning before correcting physical

Yes, sometimes we have to get physical with our horses—even with our foals. If it comes to a situation like this, do your youngster a favor and give a verbal warning about one or two seconds in advance. This gives your horse a chance to change his mind and not act out what he/she was about to do. This is the "Don't do that" cue I talked about in Chapter 6.

Always use the same word and tone of voice. A sharp "Hey," "No" or "Sst" usually does the job. Choose a word that comes naturally to you. You don't want to find yourself searching for the right word the moment you need it. These moments tend to arrive out of the blue, not leaving you much time to think!

Timing is crucial here. You must give the warning the instant you see that your youngster is about to cross a boundary—not when it already happened! If he/she still oversteps the boundary after the warning, you get physical in a way that your foal understands the message. I match the intensity the horse puts into it: big action—firm consequence; little action—little, softer consequence.

Get your point across

This means that when you ask your horse to back out of your space, that your horse actually backs out of your space! So often, people quit asking when the horse just raises its head and seems to be out of the space. If your horse's feet didn't move, you didn't get the point across! Unfortunately, talking and arguing doesn't work with horses; horses communicate better physically, especially when it comes to boundaries.

And an even more unfortunate fact is that horses are way more persistent than us! We quit a demand after a maximum of thirty to sixty seconds. Sometimes all it needs is that we keep up the demand just a little longer.

This is a very important point: always go to the end of a discussion. Don't stop halfway! Do you think your horse will take you seriously and respect you if you always stop halfway? Would you respect your boss if he were that spineless? If you decide to set a boundary, you need to see it through to the end so that your horse understands. Yes or No, this is what horses can understand—no maybes. Soon your horse will "test" the limits less and less.

It is important that you insist on the boundaries EVERY SINGLE TIME! Your horse will get confused if sometimes he is allowed to do something and sometimes not. Be consistent and be friendly.

You can imagine this relationship a bit like a bank account with deposits and withdrawals. You want to keep it balanced and always in the black. You make a deposit by doing something nice with your horse. You make withdrawals each time you have to correct your horse or do something stressful like a competition or visit the vet.

If you manage to keep this account in the plus, your horse will be more trusting and forgiving for the occasional correction, mistake or stressful event. If you happen to take out too much (go "overdrawn"), you will notice that your horse will react more defensively, fearfully and distantly.

***

We all want to feel connected with our horses and feel the magic of almost reading each other's thoughts and enjoying the time spent together. The time spent with our horse lets us forget the rest of the world, all our worries and fears. We can enjoy the now and experience blissful peace and contentment. We all long to be in this stage of relationship with our horse right away.

For whatever reason, we think if it doesn't feel like that with our horse right away, that it is maybe not the right horse, not our true soulmate. Remember, you are the creator, it is in your hands to create the relationship of your dreams with your horse. But it won't just happen overnight. Our horses aren't born with the desire to make friends with people, especially if your horse doesn't "need" you. You are the leader; you are the creator, so lead your horse with love towards your dream and make yourself important and valuable in your horse's life.

Exercise:
Your rules

You are the creator of the relationship with your horse. Go to chapter 11 in the workbook where you will find 3 key questions to think about. Answering these questions will help you build a true partnership with your horse.

If you haven't downloaded the workbook yet, you can get it here: https://www.understandingisthekey.com/workbook

---

Create a Happy Learner

Most horse owners wish that their horse always loved spending time with them. We love it when we see that our horse is happy and confident with the activity we do together. But the reality often looks different. Too often the horse doesn't seem to be motivated and is just dull, lazy, crazy and resistant. Or the horse is difficult to catch and just walks off as soon as he sees you coming with the halter. Or the horse shows a crappy attitude when you ask him to do something. And sometimes the horse just plain refuses to do what you ask him to do, like leaving for a trail ride or taking some jumps for fun.

I was exactly in this situation with my mare Mazirah. All I wanted was her enjoy our time together, but the more I "progressed" in her training, the more she showed me that she didn't enjoy it at all. I couldn't catch her, she didn't want to leave for trail rides and she constantly made that typical mare's face … you know, that face with the wrinkled nostrils and the ears slightly back—a clearly pissed expression. With her daughter Mayana, I swore to myself that I would not let this happen again. My number-one priority was to create a happy and confident learner. I wanted her to look forward to our next session and to be full of self-confidence in finding the solution to whatever I wanted her to do. And I succeeded with Mayana. She now comes when I call and sometimes even waits at the gate at the time I usually come to pick her up. It is so obvious that she enjoys our time together. She turned into a real learn-aholic.

So, how can you cause your youngster to become a happy and confident learner that finds it interesting and fun to be with you? The answer is simple: By applying the principles and strategies outlined in the Chapters 6, 7, 9 and 11 about the different Horse Personalities, Equine Learning, Creating a Plan, and Creating a Relationship. But I never said that applying those principles will be easy.

This chapter is the melting pot of those four chapters and all the principles I have outlined. I needed to share all this theoretical knowledge with you first, before showing you how to apply this in everyday practical life with your horse because everything starts with knowledge and awareness. This allows you to make smart decisions from moment to moment. And only then will you be able to set up everything you do with your youngster for success.

Using four examples of horses of different ages, I want to outline how I use all these principles every day with just one goal: To create a happy and confident learner who loves the time we spend together. But first, I need to share with you one more concept which spans like an umbrella over the whole picture.

Expanding the comfort zone

Everything your horse can do without any worry, or even without having to think much, is your horse's "blue lake,"[11] i.e., his comfort zone where he feels safest and happiest. As soon as you take your horse out of his blue lake, he will get more or less worried. If you bring your horse back to his blue lake in time, he will realize that what he just experienced wasn't that bad. The blue lake grows and so does his confidence, but if you take him out too far, you can push him over the cliff into the red zone where he might panic. This will cause the blue lake to shrink.

The young horse's blue lake is, obviously, very small. Sometimes the blue lake ends when the foal is just 10m away from his mother. For a yearling, the lake will almost certainly not include taking him out of the field away from his friends, and it will probably not include a walk in the forest on his own for your two-year-old. Maybe yes, probably not.

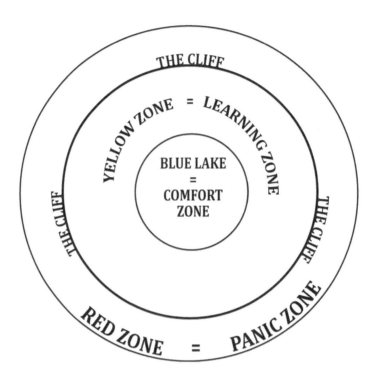

The goal of every session is to expand your youngster's blue lake so that he becomes more and more confident with everyday life in humans' world.

But this growth of confidence can only happen if you lead your horse out of his blue lake. To avoid coming close to the red zone, you need to be an expert in handling the excitement of a horse who's close to the figurative cliff edge. Pushing your horse over the cliff into the red zone will always shrink your horse's blue lake and damage your horse's confidence.

The solution is to "approach and retreat" into the yellow zone. Every time you take your horse out of the blue lake and spend some time in the yellow zone before coming back to the blue lake, your horse's confidence will grow.

Each time I take a horse out for training, I think about this concept. How far out of the blue lake is the activity I plan to do today? How can I set it up so that we don't come close to the red zone? How can I set it up so that the horse will be successful, more confident, and proud about his achievements at the end of the session?

Yes, sometimes it happens that the blue lake shrinks. Sometimes we don't manage to set everything up for success. Sometimes shit happens and things don't go at all as we expected or planned. That is part of the process. Just take note and make new decisions in the future.

To sum it up, the goal of every session is to grow my horse's blue lake, or to at least not cause it to shrink. The goal of every single session is to increase my horse's self-confidence and boldness as a learner.

To see how you can apply this to your house, here are some learning examples I set up for my horses at different ages.

Maserati: Shagya Arabian colt, 0–6 months

Maserati is the son of my mare, Mazirah, and a dream come true. I was there when he was born and witnessed his first wobbly steps and his first-time nursing. He was very shy at first, always hiding behind mommy and reacting quite shy to first approaches.

During his first month, he was turned out in a big field with his mom and stabled for the night. This gave me plenty of opportunity to socialize with him and help him form a positive association towards humans.

Main topics at this age:

- Build a positive association towards humans
- Create a solid foundation for a healthy relationship (boundaries and love)
- Nurture curiosity

Main learning strategy:

- Learning by imitation and observation of his mother
- Positive reinforcement via scratches
- Use "don't-do-this" cue to introduce on boundaries
- Approach and retreat
- Use his own curiosity to explore
- Repetition

Tasks to learn:

- Accept touching everywhere
- Accept oral medication (wormer, probiotics)
- Haltering
- Explore the world following mom
- Picking up the feet
- Basic yields to pressure
- Basic rules

Every interaction counts

Every time we interact in some way with the foal, he will learn something. At this age, the most important thing is that the foal builds a solid positive association with you and other humans. It's not really about all the tasks we teach a foal; it's more about how we are with them that leads to the desired result.

Maserati was very shy at first, even though I had been there at his birth. He was a sensitive and reactive little guy. He was super-protective about his legs, his belly, his neck behind the ears, and especially his head. First, I focused on having good contact with mom, Mazirah. I brushed her, scratched her and made her feel good. He observed us and slowly got curious about me. Soon he started carefully exploring my back with his cute little nose. It wasn't long until I could "accidentally" stroke over his neck and back. Within four days, he had found out that humans give the best scratches.

No forcing

The key was to not force contact on him, but to just allow it to happen. Foals are so curious; they just have to explore the world. If mom is confident and obviously isn't worried or even enjoys something, the foal figures it can't be bad.

During Maserati's first month, I visited him several times a day, and in the mornings and evenings, I took care of mother and foal. He went out in a field for the day and spent the night with his mom in a stall with a paddock. Often, I would just sit in the straw and wait for him to get curious and start exploring me all over.

Encourage respect

When he was about ten days old, he tried for the first time to involve me in some foal games. He would nudge me then jump away with a little happy buck. This was the first time I gently applied the don't-do-this cue and shoo-ed him away from me. I made it clear from the very first try that I am not a play buddy but would like to be respected just as he respects his mom. He never tried anything similar again as a result.

Take small steps

Slowly, I started to present new things: the halter, a lead rope, and a syringe filled with diluted honey. As he was protective about his head and felt claustrophobic quickly, I had to break everything down into mini-

mini steps. His blue lake was tiny at that time, so his learning zone was very narrow and the red zone very close. As soon as I moved a bit too quickly, or restricted him for a second too long, he would panic and fight. The next try after a situation like this was quite a bit more difficult because his confidence had shrunk.

With everything I presented to him, I just waited until he got so curious that he started to explore the object (halter, lead rope, syringe) and chew on it. This was the green light I needed to take the next mini step. When he was one month old, he was taking his first worm paste like a champ (because I had given him honey in a syringe plenty of times) and allowed me to halter him with great confidence. He loved scratches, and I could lead him around with a figure-eight rope around his body. Often I joined him for a nap in the straw—that was the best.

Explore together

A few times per week, I went for a little walk with Mazirah, Maserati following at liberty. We explored the property and our arenas with all the obstacles in them. Mazirah showed him how to walk over a tarp, the bridge, the pedestal, and how to push a big green ball. He usually became quite exuberant, galloping and bucking around. He never tried to imitate anything Mazirah did, he just observed from a distance. Danish researcher Janne Winther Christensen, PhD, showed in one of her studies that if foals observe their mother dealing with potentially difficult and scary situations, they will be braver as adults than foals that didn't have the chance to observe their mom.12

Unfortunately, at this point in Maserati's development, I had a severe accident, which stopped me from progressing with him at all. So, until he was about four months old, I was only able to visit him, sit with him in his stall. Sometimes he laid his head in my lap for a nap. These were the most precious moments.

Use positive reinforcement

While I was out of action after my accident, my husband, Thomas, visited Maserati every day in the pasture. Each time he implemented little things in a very playful and casual way into their find-the-itchy-spots session. As it was summer and we had plenty of biting insects, his ears were terribly itchy. While rubbing him all over his neck, Thomas would accidentally stroke over the ears, and it didn't take long for Maserati forgot about being ear-shy and discovered the benefit of ears scratches. Also during the visits, Thomas would rub the foal's legs and pick them up one after the other. Thomas used positive reinforcement for giving him his feet by scratching Maserati's belly while holding the foot up. This way, the foal started to give his hooves easily and also learned to stand still at the same time.

Set boundaries

Sometimes, when Maserati got too demanding for scratches, Thomas would casually back him up by the nose or the chest. Like this, little Maserati learned to yield from steady pressure and respect personal space and important boundaries, namely:

- Don't nip and don't chew on my clothes
- Don't push me
- Move out of my way when I ask
- Don't play any foal games around me or try to involve me in them

Begin "real" training

It's important to note that, until now, there have been no "sessions" of training with Maserati. Everything happened casually, whenever he was in contact with us. The only thing we focused on was building positive associations and trust towards us.

When he was about five months old, I was finally recovered enough from my accident that I could resume his education. I planned to take him out on walks, but this time not at liberty, but properly walking next to me with halter and lead rope.

To reach this goal, I first got very clear about what he already knew, including haltering, a tiny bit of yielding to pressure on the halter and going on walks. He already followed a few times at liberty on walks with Mazirah and gotten too confident during these walks, taking huge turns at the canter, exploring. So, we stopped that; it was too risky for my taste.

I absolutely wanted to avoid him being triggered by a stupid spook, start a panic and fight against halter and lead rope just because I hadn't taken the time to properly teach him how to lead.

My plan

I established the following plan to make sure that the first real walk in hand would be a good and positive experience.

1. Get him confident with weird objects in his field.
2. Teach him to follow the feel of the lead rope in all directions.
3. Teach him to lead well in his field.
4. Go for a mini walk just outside his field together with his mom.
5. Go for a bigger walk with mom but still in sight of the field and staying on the property.
6. Go for a real walk with mom and explore everything interesting on the way.

Build confidence

For step one, I took weird objects with me into the field, such as a big plastic tarp, colorful umbrellas, or even a wooden bridge. All the horses got curious, especially sister Mayana who loves to play with stuff like that. Maserati was a bit skeptical at first and observed from a distance, just like he did when he was a tiny foal, and I took him with mom Mazirah into the arena. But soon his curiosity took over and he started to imitate exactly what his sister did. Soon he played with the tarp and walked over the wooden bridge. He learned to be brave toward unknown objects simply through observation and imitation.

Repetition is key

I repeated this exercise several times. Then I went on to teach him to follow the feel of the lead rope and to lead well. He easily got claustrophobic and reacted with panic whenever anything was restricting his head. For this reason, I taught him this skill in the pasture with his family all around him. I wanted him to feel safe when learning a task that was potentially challenging for him.

I did three mini sessions of ten minutes each, teaching him how to release the pressure on the halter and how to follow the feel of the lead rope. I would quit each session when I had a confident response. Then I would cuddle and scratch him, bring him to his mom and take the halter off. He would then usually have a long drink and come back to me for more scratches.

Be attentive

I was very careful to not push him over the cliff into the red zone. I wanted his blue lake to grow at a steady rate while taking no risks. I used carefully applied pressure/feel and release and lots of rewards to teach him this. At the same time, I needed to progress quickly with him, as he is a fast learner. Too many repetitions and he would get cocky and overly playful.

Try something new

Once he understood how to follow me nicely on the lead rope, I took him on his first walk outside his usual pasture. I asked a friend of mine to lead his mother. On the first day, we didn't go very far away from their field. He knew the area, so that was nothing new to him. But as he couldn't run whenever he felt like it, he was quite a bit more tense than usual. He had to learn to relax being restricted in his freedom and trust me to take care of him.

Expand

The second time going on a walk, he already felt way more confident when leaving the field. We just explored anything interesting, like the ducks and geese, the bushes, the mailbox, the garbage bin, a stone statue, the bike parking place, and some utility vehicles of the farm. I allowed him to be curious about everything and learn by imitation and observation of his mom being brave. In a way, I was holding his hand on this adventure.

Finally, on the third session, I took him for a "real" walk of thirty minutes out of sight of the pasture. His mom was still with us. We explored a pond, jumped logs, loaded for the first time into a trailer that was on our way, and discovered the forest. Whenever he wanted to be curious about something, I encouraged him to explore. In case he lost confidence a bit, his mom was there to show him that the situation was not as scary as he thought.

Be positive

With this careful plan and set up, the first walks outside were an interesting and fun experience for him. They enabled him to associate coming out of the field with something positive. He also realized that leading is nothing restrictive; it's more like I am holding his hand to help him deal with scary situations. Since then, he has always wanted to come out of the field when I take one of his sisters for a ride, and he is super-easy and trusting when I take him for walks.

The most important thing at this young age really is to form positive associations—as many as you can. The first impressions are the ones that color a horse's perception about a certain subject for a very long time.

Tara: Shagya Arabian filly, between 1–2 years

Tara had gone through the same process as Maserati by this point. She loved to hang out with people and would always be the first to come to greet me. She was relatively easy to handle in everyday life. When leaving the herd all on her own, she stayed connected to me but got excited easily. She couldn't relax 100% when there was no other horse with her.

Her basic personality is unconfident/extroverted. This means, that I have to use a lot of consistency and reassurance and break everything down into mini steps so that she wouldn't feel overwhelmed by all the new stuff.

I only did about four sessions with her every month. Those four sessions, I did within one week for her to have the consistency she needed for her personality. Remember, it takes four to seven repetitions for a horse to learn something. Four repetitions were just perfect for her to learn a new topic. Her main difficulty was leaving the herd and being confident when being just with me.

Main topics at this age:

- Create a positive association towards leaving the herd and spending time with "her" owner/rider alone
- Get more experience with humans' world
- Master important everyday skills

Main learning strategy:

- Learning by making experiences
- Learning by imitation
- Desensitization techniques
- Repetition and routines

Tasks to learn:

- Leaving the herd
- Going for walks alone
- Yielding to pressure (advanced)
- Trailer loading (advanced)
- Fly spray and clippers
- Shower
- Advanced farrier prep
- Tying with safety

Choose a starting point

Tara was already very confident when leaving the herd with another horse together. She knew the property, the arenas, the main stables, and the grooming area. She loved spending time with me and had formed a solid positive association towards me. Now I wanted her to form a positive association towards leaving the herd on her own, just with me. This asks for a whole different level of trust for a horse her type. This is a step up from being the friend to being the guide and protector.

Be consistent

Despite being confident in some subjects, Tara was less confident and nervous in others. I created a solid routine for her that I would keep exactly the same each time. I would come in the field, call her and spend a few minutes to scratch and cuddle her. Then I haltered her in a way that she learned to put her head in the halter herself. (This is a habit I like to develop with my horses to make sure that they are really with me, even with just haltering.)

Give her time

Then I would lead her to the gate. Sometimes she would stop and not want to follow. Then I would just stop with her, give her a few seconds, rub her, and ask her to continue. If I didn't give her the few seconds, it would get worse and she got more nervous. On the way to the main stables, I took all the time she needed. Some days she would just follow me, but some days she was a bit more nervous and needed to stop several times. She is the kind of horse that accelerates rather than stops when she is scared of something. So, it was my job to watch her closely to see what she was actually scared of. I would then encourage her to stop and examine the object. Sometimes it was something obvious, like a utility vehicle. Sometimes it was just her reflection in a window. I made sure that she realized with every little scare she had that the object was harmless. I allowed and encourage her to express her fear, to let me know, and that we would explore it together. This way all her little scares eventually dissolved.

Nurture feelings of safety

Once arrived in the main stables, I positioned her in the grooming corner. She loved grooming, so standing still was no big deal for her. Here she felt safe again, and she would enjoy the special treatment. With my main goal being to help her make a positive association with spending time with me alone, I used the grooming part to really make her feel good and special. She is a little princess who loves to be pretty and fussed over.

Be casual

I took this moment to casually use the mane spray and got her used to being sprayed. Each time I practiced one or two of the utility skills. Such as cleaning and rinsing her eyes, taking temperature or the clippers.

Encourage exploring

After grooming, I would do a turn through the horse shower. I let her explore the hose and the basket with all the shampoo bottles. Once she was confident with that, I let the water run while she was exploring. This was just a little change, but for her it was major: the noise, the sparkling of the water, and the floor was suddenly two different colors. I wanted her to get completely confident with all those little things and not just manage her body and control her.

Keep it simple

The first two times I took her out alone, this was all I did. I would bring her back to her field after this. It was so easy to push her over into the red zone, and her learning zone was quite narrow.

For example, when another horse entered the stables while we were busy in the grooming corner, she would get very nervous. I could see her heart beating in her chest. If this happened, I would allow her to move and say hello to the other horse. This helped her calm down.

If I had insisted for her to stay in place, I would have triggered her claustrophobia. Remember, whenever a horse feels held and restricted in a scary situation, he/she will feel the very urgent need to run. The horse will reason that his fear isn't only about the circumstance, but you too! That's something you don't want, especially not at that age. I wanted Tara to experience me as her protector, as her guide, as her safe point. This is why I exposed her only gradually to everyday life and showed her how to deal with it.

Build on confidence

As her confidence grew, I took her on little walks. We also started to explore the arena together and look at all the objects in there. There she learned in a casual way to yield her hindquarters, to back up, to yield her shoulders and to synchronize when leading. We established some more common language. This in turn increased her confidence because she was able to understand me better.

Ask a friend to help

Now she was confident leaving the herd alone, just with me. She was confident exploring everything in and around the arena. So, I wanted to tick the next task off my list, which was trailer loading. I guess you know that this can be a very difficult task. To make it easy for Tara, I asked a good friend to accompany us with Tara's favorite nanny.

Introduce obstacles

During the first session, I went through some preps in the arena. I built up different obstacles to help Tara to deal with the trailer with more confidence later. I had the wooden bridge to simulate the noise and to increase her confidence in stepping on a different surface. I used a big blue tarp to create a tunnel that helped her gain more confidence in narrow spaces. I used a corridor of poles for her to back up through and a pole to walk backwards over.

Let her observe

At first, I allowed her to just observe her nanny confront all the challenges with ease and confidence.13 Then I would follow behind. I simply allowed Tara to be driven by her curiosity. As she saw her nanny master everything, she would quickly imitate her and do the same. Like this, I had no fear responses, no drama, no reason NOT to praise Tara and to make her feel smart and special.

In the second session, I briefly went over all the preps. This time, I asked Tara to cross all the obstacles without observing her nanny passing them first. Then I took her to the trailer. Here I asked my friend to load the nanny first, so that Tara could observe what was happening. She was very curious and tried to follow. When it was her turn to load, I simply allowed

Tara to explore the inside of the trailer. Step by step, her curiosity drove her in. I never asked or pushed/coaxed her to load, I just allowed her to be curious. Whenever she loaded all the way, I praised her quite a bit. We finished that session with me being able to load her on her own without me walking in front but standing at the entry of the trailer.

The whole setup allowed her to have a great first impression of the trailer. I could just be the encouraging guide, being there for her and celebrating when she was brave. Her little blue lake grew the most when I set up her learning this way.

Celebrate her success

At this age, it is so important that our youngsters learn to trust us as their guides, learn to see us as their protectors, and learn to have confidence when learning. At one year old, horses are very much like kids; they orientate themselves on how their herd members react and behave. What do you have to do so that he/she sees you as their favorite nanny and the guide/protector that holds his/her hoof firmly to give safety?

Gwayne: Welsh Cob filly, 26 months old

Gwayne spent two months with me because her owner started to experience some problems with her. She was basically behaving like a little bulldozer, being very pushy and invasive. When leading, she was difficult to control. Whenever she got worried or didn't want to go where she was led, she would take off, sometimes even kicking at the person on the end of the rope. The farrier didn't have a very easy time with her either, as she wasn't very cooperative having her hind feet handled. She was obviously stuck in phase two of relationship development.

During the first days of her stay, I went several times to visit her in her field. I wanted to give her time to get to know me (phase one of relationship) and to integrate into the herd that she would be living with during her stay. She met me with great confidence, right away demanding scratches and trying to walk over me at the first occasion. Gwayne showed no fear toward any equipment or when leading her from A to B. She was very "talkative" and very lively.

I evaluated her personality as a confident/extrovert. As such, her main difficulties were respecting personal space, staying in a respectful dialogue with people, her strong opposition reflex, running through pressure, and having no understanding of a healthy relationship with humans.

Main topics at this age:

- Catch up on building a healthy relationship and accepting boundaries
- Build a positive association towards learning
- Establish solid everyday routines and good habits

Main learning strategy:

- Accept boundaries
- Curiosity
- Negative reinforcement

- Positive reinforcement (verbal praise and scratches)
- Pressure and release
- "Don't-do-it" cue
- "Yes" cue

Tasks to learn:

- Solid everyday routines (standing still for grooming, giving the hooves, leading properly and with respect)
- Accept fly spray, showering and clippers
- Foundational groundwork to prepare her for her start under saddle the next year
- Trailer loading
- Going for walks alone, explore the world

Set a schedule

I decided to work with her every second day. This gave her the necessary routine she needed being a young horse. Giving her one day off between sessions avoided the risk of overloading her mentally. For Gwayne, being such a smart and confident girl, I alternated between sessions about social skills, sessions about groundwork skills, and sessions where I would take her for active walks out in our forest. She would get quite spunky if she thought things were too boring and repetitive.

Establish language

I did the first two sessions with Gwayne in the pasture. With her owner, she had acquired a habit of pulling loose when leading. I established some basic common language and cleared out the fundamental boundaries (phase 2 of the relationship). Only then would I take her out of the field and to the main stables with the grooming area and the arenas. This way, I avoided unnecessary drama and fights, which would have pushed her into the red zone.

Install routines

Then I started to install the everyday routines. When I came to pick her up, I would always spend a few minutes scratching her and haltering her in a nice way. Then I would lead her toward the main stables, 400m further. Sometimes I would play "hunt the best patch of grass" game with her.

Once arrived at the main stables, I would position her in the grooming corner. This was the perfect time to teach her to stand still without being tied while grooming. Then I would pick out her feet and take the opportunity to improve her patience when handling the hind feet. After that, I took her into the shower and allowed her to explore. She also had to learn important vet preps, such as accepting the worm paste, accepting needles, and applying eye cream. I would introduce those skills casually into our daily grooming routine—no big deal, just part of our daily routine (phase 3 of the relationship).

Challenge and reward

Then I would either go for a walk with her, practice a difficult social skill (like clippers, fly spray or trailer loading), or do some groundwork with her. I made sure to praise and reward when she put in effort and showed that she understood. She loved praise and to feel when I was happy with her! In general, I kept the sessions with her very playful and lighthearted, and she was very good at making me laugh with all her funny ideas. When I brought her back, I would always spend another two or three minutes scratching her itchy spots.

Track progress

After two months, she'd had a total of twenty-four sessions. Two were in the field, focused mostly on boundaries and basic common language. Four had been about trailer loading. Two were about clippers, fly spray, showering, and farrier preps only. Six were trail walks through our forest (positive association towards spending time with people), and ten had been sessions about foundational groundwork in the arena.

At the end of her two-month stay, Gwayne behaved politely but openly and confidently toward people. Whenever I came to pick her up, she would come when I called. She had caught up in her understanding of having a healthy relationship with people. She had learned important daily social skills and had received a solid basic education on the ground. She had also learnt to accept the cinch and saddle and was perfectly prepared for her start under saddle the following year. Gwayne had formed a positive association towards learning and spending time with people in a polite way.

Mayana: Shagya Arabian mare, age 3-4

This was the period when I started her. I gave her two five-minute rides just when she turned three years old. Then I left her alone for about eight months, except the occasional walk and some groundwork. When she turned four, I continued her start under saddle.

Mayana was unconfident and reactive to the environment. But she was also an extremely fast learner. If I didn't progress fast enough, she would be even more reactive and spooky. She switched between the unconfident/extroverted and the confident/extroverted type, sometimes within seconds. Knowing this, I knew that I had to find the right mix of consistency to improve her spookiness, but at the same time stay progressive so as to not lose her mind.

This was how I took her unique personality into account. Her main difficulties included being overly excited when leaving the herd, disliking being alone or closed in a stall, and finding it hard to concentrate. She was very explosive and jumpy.

Main topics at this age:

- Build a positive association towards work and being ridden
- Build emotional fitness
- Relaxation and willingness

Main learning strategy:

- Condition good habits through consistency
- Negative reinforcement
- Positive reinforcement
- Scan and capture techniques
- Building confidence

Tasks to learn:

- Accept cinch and saddle
- Accept rider
- Stay alone in a stall
- Advance with groundwork
- Advance with basic riding skills

Adapt to her personality

I adapted my weekly plan to her extroverted, sometimes unconfident personality. I would do five sessions per week with her. I paid attention that she had not more than one day off in a row during periods I wanted to really advance her education. This gave her the daily consistency she needed to settle into her "work." This didn't mean that I made her work physically every day; I just took her out and kept her in the routine. During her start, I would ride her every second session only as she was a very late developer. If it happened that she had two days of no "work" at all, she would be way more explosive, and it took me a lot longer to get her into a good frame of mind.

Be consistent

With this weekly structure, I respected her need for consistency in my planning. Every session followed the same routine: I would call her at the gate of her big field and wait for her to come. I spent a few minutes greeting and cuddling her. I haltered her in a way that she put her head into the halter herself.

Keep her focused on me

Then I would take her down the 400m path to the grooming area in the main stables and the arenas. Often, she felt very exuberant on this path and jumped around. Then I would play a game with her: Run, stop, back up, and graze a few seconds. This helped her to focus more on me than on her being crazy, and practice important skills along the way.

Establish everyday routines

Once we arrived at the stables with the grooming area, I would ask her to stand still for grooming without being tied. If there were other horses in the stable, I would encourage her to say hello to every horse. Her mother was pretty anxious towards horses she didn't know, and I wanted Mayana to be more confident. Once that was done, I put her in a stall with a nice pile of hay and left for a few minutes to prepare the arena and collect all my tack I would need.

Warm-up phase

When I came back, I tacked her up for whatever I wanted to do with her and took her in the arena. There I would spend about fifteen to twenty minutes with groundwork until she was calm and connected. The duration strongly depended on the mood she was in. Some days it would be thirty minutes, if she was in a particularly excited mood.

Often, she was very explosive in the beginning of the session. She was rarely with all four feet on the ground. I had to focus her mind with quick tasks the moment I entered the arena. Backing up and sideways maneuvers worked really well. Or I played with jumping some obstacles during groundwork on days when she wasn't so exuberant. Asking her to do many changes of direction when lunging, also helped her to focus more on me. I would do this until she relaxed and looked at me instead of out of the window. She was a horse who needed to move her feet to calm the mind. And only when she was calm was she ready to learn something new.

Teaching phase

In the teaching phase, I always had two skills I wanted to improve and one completely new thing. Mayana only needed three repetitions to learn something new. As she is such an intelligent and mentally active horse, I needed to advance at a quick pace, otherwise I would lose mental connection. All three tasks would be related to riding.

Improve two skills

The two skills I wanted to improve were her understanding about the rein aids (backing up and lateral flexion) and the leg aids (yield the shoulders and hindquarters, yield sideways). This took me about ten more minutes. By now, she would be relaxed, connected, and eager to do what I asked her. She was actively searching for the next praise. Then I would either ride her briefly or end the session. I was usually alternating between groundwork only and groundwork plus riding.

First few rides

When I rode her, I again had a very clear and solid plan: Repeat two things she already knew and get an improvement in them, plus teach one new task (this new task I had already introduced to her during the groundwork sessions).

The two things she already knew during her third ride were our mounting routine (come to the mounting block, stand still, lateral flexion, and backing up once mounted) and walking around the arena with confidence. The new thing was to ask her to trot. I would end the ride as soon as she would give me a few upward transitions to trot with understanding and lightness.

With this set up, I made sure that I would only ride her when she was in a positive and calm frame of mind. I never had any issues with her explosive tendencies when riding.

Cool-down phase

To end the session, I would walk her around the arena now that she was actually able to do so calmly. Maybe I would let her push the ball, which is what she absolutely loved doing. Then I untacked her completely and let her roll. Like this, she soon learned to lie down on command. When I left the arena, she was always in a peaceful and happy state and often didn't want to leave.

Then I would take her back to the stables and put her in a stall with some tasty hay. I would then leave her alone so that she would learn patience.

After about thirty minutes and only when she was calm, I brought her something nice to eat.

Awareness until the last moment

Once she finished eating, I took her back to her field. If the herd was far away from the gate, I would escort her to the herd. Like this, I avoided making her impatient as soon as I took the halter off. To say goodbye, and just after taking the halter off, I would give her a piece of carrot or some of her favorite scratches. This caused her to always stay with me after taking the halter off, rather than running back to the herd.

With the help of these four examples, I hope it is clearer to you how to apply everything described in this book in daily life. Of course, every horse if different, so every horse needs a different plan. Reflect on which plan works best for your horse. Everything interlaces and blends together. Creating a happy learner is really about acting with awareness whenever we are with our youngster. Everything we do, every moment has an impact. It's us who have the keys in our hands to set up every situation so that our youngsters can grow in confidence and expand their blue lakes.

Exercise:
What plan works for your horse?

Always ask yourself how you can set up the situation so that your horse's blue lake grows. How can you teach him to see you as friend, protector, guide, leader and as the point of safety? How can you structure your sessions with your horse in a way that your horse feels confident and successful at the end?

If you can get the answers to these questions correct, your horse will become a happy and enthusiastic learner who loves to spend time with you! Let every action be guided by empathy and love for your horse. Let your horse know when you are happy with and proud of him—this is the best motivator there is for a horse. Find out what your horse's comfort zone is and where his current learning zone is and what pushes him over the cliff. Use every moment spent with your horse to create a happy and confident learner!

In chapter 12 of the workbook, you'll find questions that can help you make your horse a happy, eager learner who loves spending time with you.

If you haven't downloaded the workbook yet, you can get it here: https://www.understandingisthekey.com/workbook

Final Words

You have reached the end of this book! I hope that the content has inspired you to create a horse that is a pleasure to be around and both easy and fun to ride. It will be a memorable and rewarding (and often challenging) journey, I can promise you that. But, in a few years, you will realize how much the two of you have grown together.

You two will know each other inside out. You will read each other's thoughts.

You will finally feel that you have the horse you ever dreamt to have. A friend.

And you created him.

Always remember: You can do more than you think you can.

You are a creator.

Do what it takes and never give up your dream … let the dream fuel the right decisions and take you in the right direction, one step at a time towards your goal. Get help when you get stuck and, when you feel desperate, remember your WHY.

Most important of it all, much more important than any technique, any theoretical knowledge is to meet your horse with your heart. Let every action be motivated by your passion for your horse, let your horse feel that you care. Let your heart guide you on this very individual journey ahead of you.

So, get to work and start creating your perfect horse!

References

Chapter 3: Leadership

Study references:

1. Konstanze Krueger, Birgit Flauger, Kate Farmer, and Charlotte Hemelrijkc, "Movement initiation in groups of feral horses," *Behavioural Processes*, Volume 103, 2014, Pages 91–101, ISSN 0376-6357, https://doi.org/10.1016/j.beproc.2013.10.007. (http://www.sciencedirect.com/science/article/pii/S0376635713002222)

2. M Bourjade, B Thierry, M Hausberger, O Petit, "Is *Leadership* a Reliable Concept in Animals? An Empirical Study in the Horse," Peking University, 2015, PLoS ONE 10(5): e0126344. https://doi.org/10.1371/journal.pone.0126344

Chapter 5: The Prey Animal

3. Irwin, Chris. *Horses Don't Lie*. Da Capo Press Inc. (Boston: 1998)

Study reference:

4. T.L. Blackmore, T.M Foster, C.E Sumpter, W Temple, "An investigation of colour discrimination with horses (Equus caballus)," *Behavioural Processes*, Volume 78, Issue 3, 2008, Pages 387-396, ISSN 0376-6357, https://doi.org/10.1016/j.beproc.2008.02.003

Chapter 6: Equine Learning

5. Jenifer A. Zeligs, PhD, *Animal Training 101*, Mill City Press (Maitland: 2014)

6. Andrew McLean, PhD, BSc, Dipl. Ed, "Principles of Learning Theory in Equitation" https://equitationscience.com/about/ises-training-principles

7. J.W. Christensen, "Early-life object exposure with a habituated mother reduces fear reactions in foals." Department of Animal Health, Welfare and Nutrition, Faculty of Agricultural Sciences, University of Aarhus, Tjele, Denmark, 2016 https://doi.org/10.1007/s10071-015-0924-7

Chapter 7: Horse Personalities

8. Lea Lansade, Faustine Simon, "Horses' learning performances are under the influence of several temperamental dimensions." *Applied Animal Behaviour Science*, June 2010

9. Linda Parelli, *Horsenalities* http://files.parelli.com/HorsenalityChart.pdf

Chapter 8: The Horse's Natural Needs

10. B.A. Hampson, M. Mills de Laat, Chris P. Pollit, "Distances travelled by feral horses is outback Australia." *Equine Veterinary Journal*, 2010, 42: 582-586. doi: 10.1111/j.2042-3306.2010.00203.x

Chapter 12: Create a Happy Learner

11. Dr Stephanie Burns, *Move Closer Stay Longer*. Navybridge Pty Limited, 2010

12. J.W. Christensen, "Early-life object exposure with a habituated mother reduces fear reactions in foals." Department of Animal Health, Welfare and Nutrition, Faculty of Agricultural Sciences, University of Aarhus, Tjele, Denmark, 2015

    https://doi.org/10.1007/s10071-015-0924-7

13. J.W Christensen, J. Malmkvist, B.L. Nielsen, L.J. Keeling, "Effects of a calm companion on fear reactions in naive test horses." Department of Animal Health, Welfare and Nutrition, Faculty of Agricultural Sciences, University of Aarhus, Tjele, Denmark, 2010

General Inspiration

Berni Zambail
Karen Rohlf, Dressage Naturally
Kalley Krickeberg
Linda Tellington-Jones
Frederic Pignon
Pat and Linda Parelli

Made in United States
Troutdale, OR
09/18/2023

12996284R00130